THE NEW
GERMAN EMPIRE

THE NEW GERMAN EMPIRE

BY

F. BORKENAU

THE VIKING PRESS · NEW YORK

1939

PUBLISHED IN AUGUST 1939

DP253
B73

CONTENTS

THE NEW
GERMAN EMPIRE

CHAPTER I

THE NAZI CRUSADE

At what is Germany really aiming?

In the light of recent events, this is a greater puzzle than ever. Before Hitler marched into Prague, a tendency prevailed to interpret German aims in the light of German official declarations. Most obviously, the German Government had repeatedly disregarded such declarations as it had made on previous occasions. Hitler guaranteed the independence of Austria, disclaimed any aspirations upon the Sudetenland, declared himself ready to guarantee Czecho-Slovakia after Munich, etc. None of these promises had been kept. Yet an impression persisted that Hitler's speeches had something to do with his intentions.

This impression was particularly strong, though particularly unfounded, in the case of Hitler's speech to the Reichstag immediately before Munich. On that occasion Hitler solemnly proclaimed that after the cession of the Sudetenland Germany had no further territorial claims in Europe. In the light of earlier disappointments, caution would have been indicated in this case more than in any other. For after Munich, Czecho-Slovakia lay helplessly exposed to German aggression, and Nazi Germany is never likely to forgo a chance of conquest. The impression made was not, however, altogether unreasonable. For Hitler's solemn pledges seemed to agree in this instance with what appeared to be the natural aim of Nazi Germany.

The national and racial idea appeared to be the crux of the Nazi faith. The logical aim of the Nazis, therefore, would be to unite all Germans in one Greater Germany. Non-Germans would not only be undesirable in a country so strongly intent upon racial purity; they would actually be driven out. Germany therefore, it appeared, could have no desire to acquire non-German populations. It is true that after the acquisition of the Sudetenland there still remained unre-

1

deemed German minorities, such as those of Memel and Danzig. That is why nobody took Hitler's pledge quite literally. But these remaining problems were insignificant as compared with the problem of Czecho-Slovakia. It was the basic assumption of the Munich policy that the era of German territorial expansion in Europe would in the main be ended with the acquisition of the Sudetenland. This, of course, was not incompatible with a great deal of German influence outside the borders of Greater Germany, especially in the east and south-east of Europe.

It seemed a logical conception; it seemed to square both with German interests and with the basic beliefs of Nazism. It was solemnly pledged by the Nazi Government. Yet Germany has gone beyond these aims and embarked upon an indeterminate campaign of expansion.

The first question which now arises is this: Were the conquest of Czecho-Slovakia and the subsequent moves of German expansion planned before Munich? In other words, was Hitler deliberately lying to Mr. Chamberlain and M. Daladier at Munich? It is a problem difficult to answer, and yet at the same time an essential one. The question is not whether Germany will now continue her course of indeterminate aggression or not. There can be no doubt that she will. The question, and a very important one at that, is whether Germany is simply carrying out well-calculated plans or is driven into limitless adventures by developments over which she herself is not the master. In the one case we must still reckon with some rational plan on the part of Germany which it would be important to discover. In the second case we are faced with an outburst of incalculable instincts which cannot but end in disaster, both for Germany and for others.

A few months ago there appeared in German an interesting study of the Nazi regime by Hermann Rauschning, former Nazi President of the Danzig Senate. This man, who participated to a degree in the closer councils of Hitler and quarrelled bitterly with him and his subordinates about German policy in Danzig, now maintains that the deepest impulses of the Nazi movement are entirely negative. "Nihilistic" he calls the spirit of Nazism. In his view, Nazism is a dissolvent of every existing conception of order, whether political, moral, or religious. But there is no real constructive aim behind this drive towards destruction. There is, in particular, no such thing as a coherent plan in Nazi foreign policy. Nazi aims are unlimited and undetermined. Recent events give colour to this view.

Rauschning does not deny—nobody could—that the Nazis have a programme. They have proclaimed their racial, national, anti-Semitic, totalitarian, and other beliefs and put them into practice. So they have done with Greater Germany; so they have tried and are trying with German domination in the South-East. But in Rauschning's view none of these aims is final, nor is there a pre-established plan of how they shall be achieved one after another. Is he right or not? It is the basic problem for the future of the world.

Perhaps a contribution to the solution of this problem can be made by analysing the several aspects and stages of Nazi expansion as it has hitherto developed. What concepts underlie these various aspects and stages? The answer will fill the greater part of this volume.

One thing, however, must be clear at the outset: it is impossible even to begin an analysis of German expansion without taking due account of the Nazi regime and its character. It is not some abstract general "Germany" which undertakes this expansion. It is *Nazi* Germany. The boundless character of Germany's present aims, and the ferocity of her methods, are both due to the Nazi regime. It is not the German people, not the broad masses, who are responsible for that policy. On the contrary, they are deeply upset by the prospect of a catastrophe into which the regime is driving the country and its inhabitants. Nazi expansion cannot be understood without at least glancing over the Nazi system itself.

There exists a widespread doctrine among historians and students of political science to the effect that the basic aims of great powers never change. By this view Nazism itself is mainly a reaction against the severe penalties imposed upon Germany at Versailles. Nazism, according to the partisans of this theory, would be bound either to disappear or to soften, once the work of Versailles had been successfully undone.

But recent events have not borne out this contention, which, moreover, is only partly and very conditionally in agreement with historical experience. The evils of the Versailles Treaty were only one incidental factor in the rise of Nazism and not at all the most important one. Since their seizure of power, the Nazis have destroyed all remnants of Versailles. It was one of those obvious aims which offered themselves to their need for expansion. But the repudiation of Versailles did not mark the boundary line of German expansion; on the contrary, it was a spring-board for further high-flung schemes. For republican and democratic Germany, the complete repudiation of Versailles would have been a glorious achievement almost beyond the scope of practical politics. For Nazi Germany it was an almost insignificant incident on the road to unlimited expansion.

Here, a historical parallel obtrudes itself. It is not the first time that the "natural" aims of a great power have proved to be no more than a spring-board for a revolutionary movement of world-wide implications. Nazism and Hitler remind us of the French Revolution and of Napoleon. In one sense the wars of the French Revolution did no more than continue the wars of Louis XIV. The old French kings had striven to make the Rhine and the Alps the borders of France, to keep Germany and Italy disunited and under their influence, and to prevent the rise of the power of Britain. The French Revolution in its wars aimed at the same things. But it coupled these rational and limited aims with a world-wide crusade for its revolutionary principles which launched it upon a campaign of world-wide conquest. That campaign carried Napoleon to Egypt, to Moscow, and to St. Helena.

On the face of it, at least, the analogy is obvious. Hitler continues the policy of the Kaiser, and if he has his way one of these years will be a new 1914. But he couples the imperialism of the Second Reich with a world-wide campaign for a new revolutionary faith which, by its very character, cannot accept the coexistence of any other faith in the world. The implication in his case, as in the case of the French Revolution, is a disappearance of all rational limits to expansion. Whether the analogy will be borne out in other aspects of the story remains to be seen.

At any rate, Germany, during the past five years, has gone, and is going at ever-increasing speed, through a revolution. Revolutions, however, have laws of their own, overriding all considerations of normal times. And there is this about revolutions, that abroad they are invariably misunderstood. It is impossible for people living under normal, i.e., non-revolutionary, conditions, to realize fully the ambience of a true revolution. Europe, in her long history, has seen many revolutions. But each time the same story has been re-enacted among those only indirectly affected through it. In non-revolutionary countries the outlines of the revolutionary process dissolved themselves in a tale of meaningless horror; or else, and this is perhaps even the more frequent attitude, the politicians of countries not directly affected by the revolutionary process regard it as a thing that really could be only a mistake, a short deviation of history, a nightmare which, once over, would lead back to the old "natural" state of things. Thus, in 1917, people believed the Bolsheviks could not last a month; in 1921, they were certain the Bolsheviks would become reasonable and harmless. They did last, but Russia became the country of mass purges.

Again, is there not a lesson here concerning Nazi Germany? There are certainly indications that the advent of Nazism broadened Germany's aims and revolutionized her methods in international policy just as much as the French Revolution did the aims of France. On the other hand, there are more than indications that in democratic countries in reality only two views about Nazi Germany have found any substantial backing: the one regards the German revolution as merely an outbreak of meaningless horror, the other as fundamentally reasonable, though tainted with certain unpleasant excesses. The partisans of the former view charge their opponents with Fascist leanings—most unjustly, I believe, in many cases. There are many sincere and even progressive democrats among those against whom such charges are levelled. The only thing which can be objected to in their point of view is that they are far too greatly imbued with the soft and reasonable atmosphere of compromise prevailing in democratic countries, and instinctively expect the revolutionaries beyond the Rhine—given sufficient time and a willingness to grant concessions— to come over to their own approach to politics. A revolution, however, is always ruthless, non-compromising, and aggressive, to the point of its own undoing.

But one must not be satisfied with historical parallels. They serve only to give a clearer idea of the underlying problem. They have here been used in order to make clearer the need for a closer examination of the character of the Nazi regime. It is no use talking about a German foreign policy in a void, as if this policy were pursued by some abstract being called "Germany" and not by a nation living in a very special and peculiar political system.

What is the German revolution? Even this basic question cannot easily be understood from the assumptions governing political life in democratic countries. Political parties in democratic countries today are usually divided roughly on economic lines. Revolutionary parties in democratic countries habitually think of themselves in terms of an economic programme, of a transfer of economic control from one class to another. The German revolution in no way corresponds to these ideas. The Nazi Party, before its advent to power, was certainly not aiming at the expropriation of the upper classes by the lower classes. In power, it has completely transformed the economic life of the country, yet one thing it did not do: it did not touch property rights except in the case of the Jews. It therefore does not fit in with current ideas of revolutions; one more reason for many to disregard its essentially revolutionary character.

There are other, less conventional approaches to the understanding of revolutions. In the case of Germany it is particularly important to analyse the peculiar stresses which brought about the Nazi revolution.

Even before the War, for reasons not to be discussed in these pages, political antagonisms in Germany were sharper than in most other countries. German socialism was much stronger than that of France, much more militant and seemingly revolutionary than that of England. German Catholicism lived at odds with the Protestant monarchy. On the other hand the paramount role of the army and the hold of the landed aristocracy over the administration had never allowed an ordinary liberal democracy to develop. Both the Right and the Left were more strongly entrenched than in France, much more strongly pitched against each other than in England. The germs of the Nazi revolution lay in the stresses of Germany's pre-War political structure.

Such a balance of forces was bound at any rate to create difficulty. Since 1914 it has been subjected to no less than four fearful shocks which, besides their political effect, shook the everyday life of every human being in Germany to the very roots.

First came the War. It was not only, as in all countries, a slaughter. It meant famine with all its terrible effects. The War ended in defeat, and famine continued for two or three years after. It broke the physical strength of the population, and made it more receptive to subsequent shocks. It heated old political and class antagonisms to fever pitch. It ended in an inglorious fall of the Hohenzollern monarchy, in the proclamation of the Republic, in what was called, in 1918, the German "Revolution." This title was more freely bestowed on the events of 1918 than on those of 1933, but corresponded much less to reality then. The "Revolution" changed very little the economic structure of the country, left the old civil service intact, restored the power of the army which defeat had dissolved, and in the main limited itself to removing princes and making parliaments the formal rulers of the country. But if the constructive result of the revolution was insignificant, its moral influence was enormous. In Germany the birthright of kings and the might of the nation had been the pivotal points of political and social life. Among the Catholic third of the nation religion successfully competed with them. But Protestantism's hold on its flock had been rapidly waning and had been, as far as it went, identified with the dynasty and the Reich. Thus revolution following upon defeat left a dead blank and, at least in the Protestant part of the country, souls craving for a faith had no other outlet left except belief in a complete change of the social order. But socialism failed them. In its extreme version it spent its forces in injudicious risings. In its moderate version it proved to be as "bourgeois" as the staunchest bourgeois themselves.

Thus, a profound crisis of all beliefs and accepted standards accompanied famine and misery. German thought has not been formed by the sceptical sense of humour of a Hume or a Voltaire. Germany is still a country with a need for metaphysics. It reacted to the complete disintegration of all existing values with an outcry for a new faith and for a saviour.

As early as 1920, after the futility of the labour movement had begun to show, Germany was in a ferment, political, religious, and economic, though no well-defined aims appeared on the surface. Upon a people in such a state of mind came down the third disaster, inflation. For the very rich it was a splendid affair. For the wage-earning classes it meant again frightful misery, but of short duration only, and therefore did not leave any profound after-effects. For all the middle classes, that solid block which had maintained the hierarchies and the values of German civilization, it meant the permanent loss of their savings which had been the basis of their peculiar kind of life. Since then, Germany has never had a real middle class. The Germans had become a nation of proletarians. And among these impoverished middle classes at the height of the inflation, Hitler in 1923 won his first sizable mass following.

The mark was stabilized again, and the years between 1924 and 1929 were a period of relative prosperity and considerable industrial progress. It appeared during these years that democracy could be worked fairly well, though only moderate Socialists and Catholics worked it with real belief and enthusiasm. But in fact both the moral and the economic roots of democracy had been cut in the previous disasters, and the frail structure could not stand a new shock. That shock, the fourth within fifteen years, came with the depression. The depression again hit the middle classes with full force, and struck the working classes to a degree and in a manner which made the situation appear hopeless. Eight million unemployed in 1932!

A correct understanding of the final act depends on the realization that the political system in Germany in 1932 was essentially what it had been in 1910. Field-Marshal Hindenburg sat in the place of the Kaiser. But in substance he held command over the same army and the same civil service, and it was the powers of these bodies which made the strength of the Reich. The strength of the Left, again as in 1910, resided in the trade unions. And the electoral forces of Right and Left were as nicely balanced as they had been in 1910. As in 1910, no parliamentary majority could be found without the support of the Catholic Party, which alternately backed the Right and the Left and aptly called itself the Centre Party. Every economic status, every political and moral value, had been revolutionized in the meantime. But the party system had remained unchanged and in a state of deadlock.

The Nazi revolution of 1933 was directed against this deadlock. It was not a class movement. It drew its recruits from the discomfited and despairing of all classes. After so many disasters, no one any longer believed in the capacity of the old party machinery to bring help and remedy. Conservatives and Progressives were equally discredited. The young generation laughed at the lingering ideals of their elders, whether conservative or liberal democratic. The outcry was for an absolute ruler who would remove all the obstacles blocking the way to recovery and overcome all those who dared to resist him. The Nazi Party was fundamentally not a party with a definite programme, pledged to definite measures. Its programme consisted essentially of two points: belief in the Führer and claims of unlimited powers for him.

Thus both the conservative and the advanced forces of the past were swept away. True, Hitler had to slip into power with the help of the conservatives, because he could not hope successfully to fight the armed forces of the State. But this collaboration with the conservatives was a passing episode, ending in their discomfiture and destruction. Here for the first time, as so often later, Hitler succeeded in convincing his natural enemies that he was really their friend and that they had nothing to fear from him—only to ruin them afterwards. The process of crushing the Right has been slower under Nazi rule than the one of crushing the Left. But the result has been the same in both cases. All the political forces of the past have been wiped out.

It is meaningless to ask whether Nazism is a socialist revolution against the old ruling classes or a reaction of the upper classes against the threat from the masses below. With the advent of Nazism, a political body recruited from all classes but independent of them all has taken power into its hands and established its absolute domination. It has been left to circumstance in what direction the new regime would move. Nothing in its structure compelled it to submit or even to listen to the wishes of any section of the people.

Whoever would understand the trends of present German politics must start from this clean breakaway from the past as the essential fact. Hitler and his party came into power not because of any point in their programme, not even anti-Semitism. They rose as a result of the complete disintegration of the old economic structure and of the old spiritual values in Germany. In their stead the belief now stands that Hitler is the chosen saviour of the German people, destined to lead it to some indefinite glory. Hitler probably thinks of himself only as an instrument of God for his people, but as far as they believe in him there remains no room for the worship of any other god but him.

It is a revolution very different in kind from others. Its tenets bear no comparison with the limited, well-defined demands raised during the English Revolution, and even compared with the "liberty, equality, fraternity" of the French Revolution and its various embodiments in statutory and constitutional law, the present German Revolution will inevitably appear half a mystical and half a meaningless event. A mystical undercurrent, a belief in the coming of the millennium, can certainly be traced in every revolution and usually provides justification for all the horrors which are bound up with it. But in the case of Germany this quasi-religious fanaticism has swallowed up every concrete and well-defined aim. The German Revolution is therefore under the guidance not of a political but of a prophetic movement.

This is not to say that it is lacking in shrewdness, astuteness, and political calculation. On the contrary, the claim of a supernatural mission, however vaguely defined, works as an endorsement for the disregard of ordinary morals. But this concerns only means. The aim is not practical in any definite sense. It is, we repeat, prophetic.

A political movement, if it is to keep its following together, must be able to point to a reasonable amount of achievement in the direction of its practical programme. A prophetic movement need not stoop to insignificant achievements in the practical sphere. It can ask from its followers and impose upon them a tremendous amount of self-sacrifice for the sake of achieving its supernatural glory. But the prophet, while rid of many of the considerations of common sense, is under one terrible obligation: he must work miracles. If he does not, he is no longer a prophet. It is the only point where he is dependent on public opinion. But it is a decisive one. Neither force nor commonplace success will help him if he fails on that score. Besides, Hitler himself is an intensely prophetic personality and, like every prophet, could not exist without experiencing himself his magical powers. The craving of the Führer and of his following works in the same direction.

The query whether the Nazi regime could return to normalcy is therefore quite meaningless. Normalcy has no place in the sphere of prophetic revelation. Prophecy is the contrary of common sense. If common sense prevailed, the regime would be useless and meaningless and cease to exist.

There is something very peculiar about the particular kind of prophecy contained in Nazism. Even as a prophecy it is vague and indefinite. The belief in the Nordic race is something quite artificial, a sort of ideological superstructure with little emotional appeal; witness the personal type of the Führer himself which corresponds so little to the official Nordic ideal. And besides the Nordic faith, there is nothing but the faith in the Führer. Normally, prophets arise in the name of some god different from themselves whose message they have to transmit. This is not so with Hitler. His prophetic mission has no other content than his own person. He must play the role of the prophet and of the Messiah in one.

It is therefore only natural that the Nazi programme, so vague and indefinite in its positive tenets, should be extremely precise in its negative aspects. Everything except absolute subordination to the Führer is satanic. The real Nazi programme consists of "antis." The Nazis are anti-liberal, anti-democratic, anti-parliamentarian, anti-conservative, anti-Marxist, anti-Catholic, and anti-Christian in general, and primarily, of course, anti-Semitic. There is nothing like anti-Semitism to reveal the true character of the Nazi movement. The Jews, a small and helpless minority, are no real enemies at all. But that is just what makes anti-Semitism so essential for the Nazis. A real enemy might be defeated and disappear, and once this had been achieved the prophetic mission would be at an end. The figure of the Jew as the embodiment of all forces of the dark is eternal, precisely because the figure has nothing in common with reality. It is nothing but a straw puppet for prophetic aggression.

Thus anti-Semitism reveals some of the most important features of the Nazi movement with a direct bearing upon its attitude in the international field. It reveals that aggression is an intrinsic feature of Nazism. Without aggression and without the belief of being the object of aggression Nazism would never survive. It is not the result of some inferiority complex which might be smoothed out by adequate treatment. It is intrinsically bound up with the movement itself. But there is this peculiarity about Nazi aggression, that it never attacks a stronger or an equal enemy. For in a fight against equals miraculous success can by no means be taken for granted, and the adventure might easily end in the prophet's disgrace. Nazism must go on struggling indefinitely, but it must never be a real fight between real forces capable of joining combat. Nazism always strikes the helpless and does not strike them before they have become helpless. It is a crucial point for the understanding of Nazi foreign policy.

Here Nazi tactics are indissolubly linked with the basis of the movement itself. A prophet carrying a supernatural message needs only to prove his prophetic quality by signs and symbols. But a prophet aiming to be himself the Messiah and to bring immediate salvation to this world must make his earthly career a constant sequence of miraculous successes. And as this world is, this cannot be achieved by means of a straight fight against straight adversaries.

But there is more. It is not only the peculiar nature of the Führer's prophetic claims, it is just as much the reality of the German situation which makes a return to normalcy a hope impossible of achievement. We have seen how Hitlerism was the outcome of tremendous stresses in a situation of political stalemate, and of the reaction of the masses against it. The Nazi regime, by suppressing the right of organization and of free expression, has prevented these stresses from expressing themselves in the ordinary forms of political battles. But those stresses, those economic difficulties and sufferings, those sectional interests and antagonisms, have not been wiped out by the advent of Nazism. They have only been bottled up without any normal outlet. The form of the difficulties and stresses has been changed under the Nazi regime, as we shall see in the next chapter, which deals with Nazi economic politics. But the substance of poverty, destitution, malnutrition, overwork, and insecurity has remained and in some respects even increased. Germany today is a boiling cauldron without a safety valve. The regime itself in its need of finding miraculous cures for very serious but commonplace difficulties has augmented the pressure. And the only question is in which direction the cauldron will explode. This is the only thing the regime in all its apparent strength can really attempt to control. For explosion there must be. A prophetic regime cannot in the long run allow its following to realize that life is just as drab or even drabber than it has ever been.

As the Nazis have no definite programme, they can more or less freely choose the direction of the onslaught they started. They may attack any section of their own people or any suitable adversary in the foreign field. But of course no such attack, however ruthless and however successful, will be able finally to solve the problem. Therefore the attack is inevitably directed in turn upon every available object. There exists a definite connexion between the measure of tension inside Germany and the aggressiveness of the regime both at home and abroad. Aggression at home and aggression abroad can work as substitutes for each other. Yet there can never be an end to aggression as a whole, because it is not determined by any real grievance but by the prophetic character of the regime and the tension which this very character is creating inside the country. The views of the Gestapo about the feelings of the people are therefore more important for German foreign policy than any facts of international affairs proper, however important in themselves.

It must be borne in mind also that the reactions of a prophetic totalitarian regime to difficulties are exactly the contrary of the reactions of a common sense liberal regime. A liberal country when faced with serious difficulties at home inevitably becomes weaker in the international sphere. For a totalitarian regime growing difficulties at home are only a reason for growing aggression, to the point of desperate ventures.

There are no definite aims and no definite limits to Nazi expansion, for it is not directed fundamentally towards the removal of any real grievance or the destruction of any real enemy. It moves in an atmosphere of unreality and of a chase after the miraculous which cannot be transformed by any changes in the field of objective reality. All practical aims are subordinate to this supernatural urge.

But this does not mean that the regime cannot deal with practical problems. On the contrary, the terrific momentum and the disregard for ordinary morals which characterize the movement help it tremendously in achieving practical aims. The German Revolution in its expansion abroad is even bound to solve, incidentally as it were, a great many practical problems. But no limited solution can still the insatiable hunger of this Moloch. Every new victim serves merely to stimulate its appetite.

Besides, the movement is living in an atmosphere of self-created dangers. The prophet has not really proved himself so long as people are living happily outside his dispensation. What is the use of defeating Catholicism and Christianity in general inside Germany when they remain world powers abroad, proving by their very existence the limits of the power of the new Messiah? What conviction does the defeat of liberty and democracy in Germany carry so long as they regulate the life of other great nations? What importance has the defeat of German communism so long as the Soviet Union exists? The new faith must embrace the whole world or the validity of its prohetic claims will be disproved. Liberalism, a system of tolerance, can easily put up with the existence of anti-liberal creeds abroad as well as at home. But a Nazi creed must be all-embracing in order to be valid. We will meet that situation step by step as an essential element in German foreign policy. A liberal regime would be untrue to itself in accepting ideological wars. But the Nazi Messiah and his following can exist only in the form of a permanent crusade.

CHAPTER II

NAZI ECONOMICS AND GERMAN EXPANSION

WE must now get a step nearer the immediate problems facing Nazi international policy. It is true that all these problems, important as they are, are overshadowed by the inexhaustible need for expansion. Yet certain problems of a practical nature, especially economic ones, oblige the regime to take immediate action, and therefore at times are more in the foreground than the deeper ideological and religious impulses. In the long run the Nazis must prove the validity of their prophetic faith and attempt to destroy all other forms of life. But these are tasks which can be achieved gradually and allow of delay and procrastination. The economic needs, however, were urgent from the first day of the regime onwards, and not for a single moment was there any escaping them. When the Nazis came into their own in February 1933, they were confronted with a statistical unemployment of six millions and a real one of probably more than eight. The young generation of the working classes had never seen a factory from the inside. And hundreds of thousands of business people were ruined. It was this disaster which had finally brought the Nazis into power. They could not have kept it without finding a remedy for unemployment. It was their most urgent task. On the advent of the Nazis unemployment figures had not yet begun declining from their peak, but business was already recovering slowly both in Germany and abroad. The new regime conceivably might have entrusted itself to the natural business trend, stimulating it by State orders within the ordinary financial capacity of the country.

But this course was for various reasons unattractive to the regime. At best it would have led to a recovery, followed in a few years by a business recession. There would have been nothing staggering and sensational in that, nothing likely to justify the extraordinary claims and powers of the regime. The recovery was bound to be limited.

16

German prosperity before the Nazis depended very largely on exports and therefore on the world market, and Germany had found it very difficult to export sufficiently even during the preceding boom. Then, the effects of natural recovery would have been very gradual, and big business would have profited from it much earlier and much more thoroughly than the masses for whose allegiance the movement had primarily to care. The regime felt the need of doing something very big immediately. Finally, a policy of letting things go their way thoroughly disagreed with the temper of the Nazi movement as a whole, with the belief that a new saviour could completely abolish suffering by his mere will. So, any idea of a liberal trade policy was discarded.

Currency inflation might have provided an alternative solution. It would have made it easier for Germany to force exports, and at the same time the State, by creating new money, might have given out big orders to industry despite the scarcity of the sources of taxation at the moment of a terrific slump. Controlled devaluation of the currency would not even have been wildly unorthodox, at any rate not more so than what Britain and the United States had done before. But horror of inflation lay in the bones of the German masses, and for that reason it would have been difficult to keep the depreciation of the currency within limits and to avoid a wholesale flight into foreign currency. A currency devaluation would have been the most unpopular of all measures, bound to unite the whole people against the Government. The Nazis could not run such risks in the beginning.

The new regime, therefore, at first limited itself to patchwork: a limited amount of public works, the introduction of labour camps, the elimination of women from productive work, etc. But from the end of 1933 onwards, rearmament suddenly provided a large-scale solution.

From an economic point of view, rearmament combined several advantages. It permitted a rapid increase in the number of workers; but since armaments represent an unproductive outlay, it did not increase the national income, and did not threaten inflation. The secret of Nazi economic policy is that everyone is working much more than in 1933 but consumes only a very little more than at the worst of the depression. The number of working hours today is considerably above that of the best days of the boom in 1929, but the amount of consumable goods produced lies still far below that figure. The total of wages paid in Germany is of course higher than at the advent of the Nazis in 1933, for there are perhaps ten million more at work and the working day has been expanded from eight to ten or twelve hours. But amidst rekindled furnaces and an actual scarcity of labour the real wages of the individual worker are a good deal below even the starvation wages of 1932. While there is no unemployment, the "winter help" originally created for the sake of the unemployed is lustily continuing to work, filling the empty stomachs of labourers working at starvation wages with charity soups. Profits, on the other hand, have been rigorously limited to six per cent, and the State by taxation and forced loans is taking the surplus.

This system has been so repeatedly described as not to need further elaboration. It obviously can work only with the help of the most rigid control of the whole economic life. Otherwise wages, prices, and profits could not be kept down and inflation would inevitably ensue. For the financial starting point of German rearmament was not different from that of any other measure of creating employment by State help out of sources other than the ordinary revenue. Originally, rearmament was financed by State-issued short-term discountable "work creation" notes for which there was no sufficient cover in the treasury. Normally, the issue of these unfounded loans with the subsequent increase of money in circulation would have made wages, prices, and imports rise without increasing exports correspondingly, thus upsetting the balance of trade and finally devaluating the mark itself. This was prevented by the simple device of *not* allowing wages and other classes of income to rise. The all-powerful Nazi State, after having destroyed the trade unions and the various organizations for the safeguarding of industrial, agrarian, and banking interests, could afford to impose its law upon all classes of the population. Wages were fixed by decree at the lowest level; prices in a similar way, and the money which was thrown into circulation through the issue of "work creation" notes was withdrawn again by taxation, to be issued again for further rearmament.

With all classes of incomes artificially kept down, imports of goods for consumption could not possibly have risen very considerably. But the German balance of trade was an extremely sensitive thing. German holdings abroad were small, and the country on the whole had to pay for her imports out of her exports. There was a considerable burden of foreign indebtedness, too. Reparations had come to an end in 1932, but there remained the "frozen credits" of industry and public bodies which went into thousands of millions. They derived from heavy German borrowing abroad during the boom and waited for repayment until such time as recovery would set in. In these conditions even a small increase of German imports was apt to upset an uneasy balance of trade and to threaten the mark. And even the strictest measures of the Nazi regime had not succeeded in preventing some increase of demand from taking place in response to the enormous increase of employment. Some additional demand for foreign goods was bound to arise from that score. And an enormous increase of these demands arose out of rearmament itself.

Rearmament naturally was not only an economic measure. Though it had really to a considerable extent arisen primarily as a means of dealing with economic distress, it was from the first moment meant as a serious political measure as well. At home, rearmament going together with conscription (which in its turn relieved the labour market) helped to create that atmosphere of a state of war which suited the regime. Aimed in the first place at a redress of the grievances of the peace treaty, it took up one of the most outstanding slogans of the party and helped to carry it into practice. Finally it created a basis for that policy of unlimited expansion which was a fundamental objective of the regime. Thus rearmament satisfied the craving of the workers for a job and the craving of the young people of the middle classes for national glory, and so merged in the work for one aim the two groups who had previously been most bitterly hostile to each other—a real stroke of genius.

But in order to achieve its aims in the field of foreign policy, rearmament had to proceed at top speed. First the task was to get adequate armament before the western powers became fully aware of the danger and took action to stop it in the beginning. Then, rearmament had to proceed at such a pace as to reach and overreach the arms of Germany's potential adversaries before they in turn began seriously rearming. At present, German rearmament must keep pace with the rearmament of nations financially much stronger than herself. Thus rearmament in Germany was carried out *in furioso*, in the hectic atmosphere of the Nazi regime and contributing in its turn to it. The whole nation had to make enormous sacrifices for its sake.

For while the Nazis were perfectly able to fix prices, wages, and incomes at home, the pace of rearmament was one of the things over which they did not have complete control. If they had failed to bring it about at the pace actually achieved, it would have failed in its political purpose. All other economic considerations had to be subordinated to the needs of rearmament.

This made the problem of the German trade balance very acute. Germany is not a naturally rich country. In years of bad harvests it has, despite Nazi efforts to increase the agricultural yield, a heavy deficiency of cereals. It has a constant deficiency of dairy products. It is almost totally deficient in all raw materials for the textile industry. It has no rubber. And except for coal and potash, of which there is a surplus, it has only insignificant quantities of any mining product including iron ore. Germany is reduced to buying the wherewithal of her nutrition and her industrial process abroad and to procuring the foreign currency by exports. And this need increases with every expansion of her industrial apparatus. It increased enormously with the beginning of rearmament.

Here, incidentally, lies the decisive natural difference between Germany and Russia, whose regimes present so many parallels in other respects. The Soviet Union finds almost every raw material she needs in sufficient quantities within her own borders. Once her natural wealth has been opened up, her chief need is for finished products. And this need diminishes with every progress of industry. Every extension of production makes Russia more independent of outside contacts, more self-contained, and in a sense less aggressive. Germany, on the other hand, with every extension of her plant, becomes more dependent upon foreign raw materials, more closely linked to the chain of world trade, and therefore more aggressive if she cannot get by ordinary trading what she needs.

Now it is precisely difficulties of this kind that have arisen out of the policy of rearmament. Germany cannot make her exports (by means of normal trade) meet her additional needs for the import of armament raw materials. Hence the absolute need for a strict control of foreign trade. In order to overcome her difficulties, Germany has cut down to the lowest margin all imports other than those necessary for rearmament. The saying that Germans today are getting "guns instead of butter" has become famous. On the other hand, Germany does whatever she can to force her exports by means of State subsidies and State-enforced dumping. But neither the one nor the other measure is adequate to the task.

As a result, the outcry for "autarchy," for self-sufficiency, was raised. Germany ought as much as possible to get rid of her international trade entanglements and produce what she needs within her own borders. Much has been done in the line of finding substitutes for foreign raw materials. Some of the experiments concerned date back to the war and sometimes, as in the case of the manufacture of saltpetre out of nitrogen, have been staggeringly successful. But on the whole this policy has its fairly narrow limits. Substitutes are mostly inferior in quality to the original product and therefore cannot be used in rearmament, though they can well be used for consumption goods. The process of production is invariably costly, demanding more labour than the production of the original raw material. And this at a certain point becomes prohibitive in a country such as Germany, where, owing to the pace of rearmament, shortage of labour is acute. Besides, no such device could ever help to reach a final balance between exports and imports. For German rearmament has started a terrific international armament race which puts constantly increasing strains on all countries and primarily on Germany. Rearmament, like the Nazi movement in general, is a never-satiated Moloch. The demands not only for raw materials but also for human labour are ever increasing. But the demand for German goods abroad is very inelastic and subject to trade recessions and political dislike of Germany.

The policy of self-sufficiency is in acute conflict with the basic natural conditions existing within the borders of the present Reich. If Germany is to become self-sufficing, she ought first to become a country like Russia with an almost unlimited natural wealth, a huge population, and an enormous birth-rate. As she is, she is more dependent upon international trade connexions than many other countries and can less afford additional strains. She must choose between two extremes. She can put up with her dependence on international markets and keep her production within the limits of the opportunities provided by her exports. But that would imply renouncing the aim of keeping ahead, in the rearmament race, of powers financially stronger than herself. If she does not want to do that, she must get direct control of the raw materials she needs. In other words, she must expand and conquer.

It should never be forgotten that German needs are indefinitely expanding. In her race for superior strength she needs ever-increasing amounts of labour, food, raw materials, and foreign exchange. As in other respects, so in this there can never be a point of satiation. Given the policy of rearmament, self-sufficiency is Germany's most urgent need. But precisely because of this policy, self-sufficiency can never be attained. The solution of this contradiction lies in constant expansion.

Thus rearmament, undertaken partly as a miraculous device against all evils of unemployment and partly as a means of enhancing Germany's power and prestige, does in its turn create a real need for more power and for the control of greater economic resources. It is a vicious circle where the desire for conquest produces the need for conquest.

The problems and strains existing inside Germany on the advent of the Nazi regime have been transformed without being removed. Unemployment has given place to labour shortage, which means overwork. The unsaleable stocks of the period of depression have not only disappeared; they have given way to an acute shortage of goods and to the deterioration of their quality. Instead of unemployment there is extreme underpayment, and instead of a strangling dependence upon world markets there is rearmament carrying with it the actual need for expansion and aggression. The Nazi movement under the pressure of the sufferings it creates at home and of the tension it creates abroad can never find a balance, a place to rest, a point of saturation.

At present, in the initial stages of her period of expansion, Germany is torn between her need for foreign goods and her need for self-sufficiency. The obvious solution is to find a trade policy where foreign goods can be had without affecting the trade balance. The barter agreement which Germany aims at making the prototype of her trade agreements is a device for bringing about that aim. Germany has very little foreign exchange to pay for foreign goods. She must try to get them without paying in gold or gold value. Barter eliminates the money element from the transaction.

It is impossible at this point to abstain from some comment on the far-reaching implications of these methods for the economic system. A system eliminating gold from its most essential sphere, that of international trade, can obviously have very little in common with what is generally called a capitalist regime. In a capitalist regime prices are fixed by competition in the market, and gold is the ultimate means of expressing them. It still is so in such countries as Britain, United States, and France. It no longer is in Germany; just as little as in Russia. There exists in Germany as in Russia a medium of circulation called "money" on grounds of tradition, but it has no part in fixing values. All prices and all sources of income in Germany are essentially fixed, not by competition but by the State. As there is no free trade, there is no business cycle, no booms, and no slumps. The State, in Germany as in Russia, can always order things to be produced at its pleasure, and can distribute the products at its will.

It is certainly not a state of things such as socialist labour movements aim at. While there exist economic inequality and economic privileges, they are brought about not by the laws of the market but by the will of the State. The difference between the type of inequality and the type of economic privileges existing in Russia and in Germany is considerable. We cannot here enlarge upon this subject and must limit ourselves to the statement that distribution in Germany as in Russia is regulated by the State, but on different lines.

The essential aim of barter is to extend the sphere of this system of production beyond the political borders of Germany. Barter as in the agreements concluded between Germany and other countries is not barter between individual business men on one side and another. On the contrary, all barter agreements rigidly exclude private trade and that by at least two distinct methods. On the one hand it is the Governments themselves who are bartering. If Rumania sells a certain amount of oil to Germany and gets typewriters in exchange, it is the Rumanian Government which undertakes to procure the oil and the German Government which undertakes to provide the typewriters. Payment to the ultimate private producers is in both cases made by the State banks concerned. Moreover, and this is at least as important, barter agreements tend not even to be concluded for definite quantities of goods. Germany aims at buying up in advance entire crops and entire mineral outputs of certain kinds, and sometimes barters against them compound services such as road-building and town-planning which cannot be calculated exactly in advance. In agreements of this kind the goods and services mutually exchanged have no longer the character of calculable economic values at all. If Germany buys the whole of the Bulgarian tobacco harvest, it is exactly the same as if she requisitioned the whole excess over the producers' own consumption of the German tobacco harvest and compensated the producers with other goods or State services.

In a sense the system is ideal. Yet there is a flaw in it. Germany needs the raw materials and foodstuffs of many countries who would be glad to barter them against industrial goods. But those industrial goods Germany cannot supply, being fully engaged on rearmament. The exchange of Yugoslav wheat against German aspirin is a caricature so long as Germany, as some wit said, cannot supply a sufficient number of headaches at the same time. Barter between Germany and other countries is constantly struggling against difficulties of this kind.

We shall have to say a little more about these problems when discussing German trade with her various vassal countries. But some general facts are better mentioned here. The difficulties that Germany encounters in her own industrial production make it very difficult for her to keep up her export trade. And this again makes it very difficult for countries bartering with Germany to get from her what they really need. The barter agreements, therefore, tend to be bad bargains for the countries concerned. These countries are obliged to trade with Germany because she is one of their biggest customers, and cannot trade with her otherwise than by barter or barter-like forms of exchange. But they naturally tend to limit the extent of their bartering with Germany to a level where they remain free to carry on normal trade with other countries. But if countries bartering with Germany are able to find other outlets for their goods, this strengthens their position in negotiating with Germany. And Germany is not so much unwilling as unable to provide those industrial goods most urgently needed by many of the countries concerned. If Germany is to get the sort of trade she needs, she must first substantially control the economic life of the countries with which she is trading.

Here is the point where economic expansion is inevitably bound up with political domination. The barter agreements Germany can offer are in most cases not such as would be accepted by a country free to determine her own trade policy. In order to get her way, Germany must control those countries both politically and economically. She must try to cut them off from their foreign markets. She must try to become the master of their supplies without offering proportional advantages in exchange. In other words, she must make these weaker countries objects of economic exploitation, and in order to maintain this state of things must get control of their Governments. Germany's trade with the countries of South-Eastern Europe and with Latin America tends to be not so much a form of exchange as a form of acquiring colonies for economic exploitation. This must be so even if Germany were not ridden by an inexhaustible urge for domination. It is a direct result of her incapacity to deliver in sufficient amounts textiles, engines, and similar staple commodities of the kind and quality required.

In order to overcome the situation, Germany will have to expand her industrial production. This she is already doing but only for the sake of keeping up the armament race. It is a task which exhausts all her resources. If she wants to supply, say, textiles to all her tributary nations, she will not be able to produce them in sufficient quantities within her own borders. She will have to get them elsewhere. In other words, if Germany seriously intends to control the economic life of many of the food- and mineral-producing countries, she will have to draw modern industrial countries into the orbit of her economic system in order to provide for the industrial needs of the producers of raw materials. The annexation of the Sudetenland is a first step in this direction.

Even in purely economic matters it is a mistake to think of Germany as following a programme of limited expansion. Owing to the armament race, her balance of trade is bound to remain under a constant threat. She could remove that threat only by bringing under her control all the essential raw materials she needs. But that in itself implies a policy of world-wide expansion. Moreover, she cannot control all essential resources of any country without providing all its essential needs. So every extension of Germany's domination over the producers of raw materials carries with it the need for domination over industrial countries, which in its turn creates an additional need for foodstuffs and raw materials, and so on. It is not really a vicious circle, it is only a constantly widening one because no final balance between the supply of raw materials and of industrial goods can ever be struck.

The natural facts underlying this situation are not produced by the German system. Two countries or groups of countries could never mutually supply all their essential needs. In a free-trade system these deficiencies are automatically smoothed out. Trade between two countries under free-trade conditions does not usually balance, and one of the two always remains with a surplus of free exchange which is used for covering other needs in other countries. But it is precisely this free exchange which Germany lacks, and it is owing to this lack that she attempts to conclude barter agreements.

In order to realize the full implications, one must remember that some of the essential raw materials come from as far as Mexico, Brazil, and Malaya, whereas these countries in their turn are supplied with industrial goods from all over the world. Germany's need of political-economic expansion is therefore absolutely limitless. She wants to keep up the highest standard of industrial efficiency. Therefore she cannot dispense with the products of the farthest corners of the world. Her economic system prevents her from buying them. The only solution for her is to conquer them.

9/12/39

CHAPTER III

AUSTRIA AND THE SUDETENLAND

AFTER having given an outline of the driving forces behind Nazi expansion, we must consider its various objectives. For this we take Munich as a starting point, however much out of date it may appear at present. It may now seem artificial to discuss the Sudetenland under one heading and the remainder of Czecho-Slovakia under another. But the division is not so artificial as it may appear. There exists a deep difference between Austria and the Sudetenland on the one hand and the remnant of Czecho-Slovakia on the other. The former are inhabited by Germans, and can be regarded now as integral parts of Greater Germany. The latter is inhabited by non-Germans, anti-Germans, and can never be anything but an area ruthlessly oppressed and exploited by its conquerors. The type of regime is different in the two cases.

Moreover, the conquests up to Munich belonged to a general conception different from those which followed. Up to Munich, Germany took a stand on the right of self-determination. This principle of self-determination not only defined and limited her aims; it provided in addition certain guiding lines for her dealings with the smaller nations of Europe. The principle of self-determination excluded direct conquest. It did not exclude indirect rule. Germany, before the march into Prague, was obviously aiming at the creation of a vast empire by methods of indirect rule. She could rule all the smaller European nations without actually conquering them.

Indirect rule is always based on a nice balance between force and consent among the subject races. With the march into Prague, Germany has thrown overboard her policy of winning the consent of her future servants. The policy of indirect rule—which will be more closely defined in later chapters—has received a death-blow at Prague. From the period of diplomatic manœuvring for supremacy, we are now rapidly moving towards conquests by main force. But that is not to say that all traces of the previous method have already been wiped out. There remain many important countries, such as Scandinavia, the Netherlands, Switzerland, etc., where the policy of main force has not yet been adopted and where the old methods of peaceful permeation continue, though they carry much less conviction now than before.

Finally, the query raised in our introductory chapter remains: Could Germany build a wide empire on the principle of self-determination of nationalities and on the methods of indirect rule?

In order to answer this query, and the other problems just mentioned, we must still take our stand on the situation created by the Munich agreement. Looked at from this angle, German expansion falls easily under two headings: on the one hand there are Austria and the Sudetenland, already acquired by Germany by right of self-determination; on the other hand, there are the unredeemed territories which Germany could still claim by this right. But Germany, even before the march into Prague, did raise claims not only for territory inhabited by Germans but for territory previously belonging to Germany but inhabited by non-Germans. This was the case with such territories as the Polish Corridor and North Slesvig. We shall deal with these territories together with the unredeemed German-speaking regions.

Austria and the Sudetenland, harbouring together more than ten million inhabitants, require a separate study. In the case of the other German claims, the indirect consequences are much more important than the direct value of their acquisition. We shall therefore deal first with Austria and the Sudetenland in themselves, then with the remaining German claims (as they stood before the march into Prague) and all their implications, and only then turn to the wider German aims in Eastern and South-Eastern Europe and outside Europe. For it is in the sphere of these wider aims that the rapid transition from the pre-Munich to the post-Munich policy of Germany becomes most apparent. Especially in the east and south-east the transition from the policy of self-determination and indirect permeation to the policy of main force can be studied. But before the new method is studied, the old one must be well understood.

Turning to Austria and the Sudetenland, we must first repeat that they are united to Germany by the bond of a common language, and it is on this ground that Germany claimed them. The principle on which Germany took her stand in these cases is not quite the same as the principle of self-determination proclaimed by President Wilson in 1918. Wilson maintained that every population should, in principle, go to the country to which she wished to belong. Germany maintains that all Germans must belong to the Reich whether they want it or not. But after all, a language tie is a very close link in our times. Many anti-Nazis, when faced with the dilemma of escaping Nazism and remaining outside the Reich, or joining the Reich under Nazi domination, may choose the latter. Even if they resisted the process, they would be more ready than non-Germans to put up with the *fait accompli* of German annexation.

Yet these ties of common language are not absolute and all-inclusive. Other loyalties may cut across them, especially where German-speaking regions in their previous history belonged to distinct political units with a strong individuality of their own. This was emphatically the case in the two regions hitherto acquired by Germany—Austria and the Sudetenland. Both of them had been parts of the old Austrian Empire and as such had belonged to the Holy Roman Empire until 1806, and again to the loose German Confederation between 1815 and 1866. But they had always been more closely connected with the non-German parts of Austria than with the Germans outside Austria, and since 1866 had not been part of the Reich at all. Among the Germans of the Austrian monarchy there existed strong resentment against the Prussians who ruled the new Reich.

How far did Nazi Germany overcome this resentment? She was certainly better fitted to do it than the old Prussian Reich. It is a misconception to regard Nazism as a new edition of Prussianism. The Führer himself is an Austrian, and very few of his staff are Prussians.

The army, the embodiment of Prussia's rule over Germany, has been deprived of its political influence. The prophetic and propaganda spirit of the regime is utterly incompatible with the dry sense of duty and of silent obedience which was the core of Prussianism. The Nazi regime is thoroughly plebeian, whereas in old Prussia the aristocracy ruled. The Nazi regime is therefore much nearer to the Germans outside the borders of the Reich than the old Prussian system ever was.

On the other hand, inside old Austria itself there existed strong trends hostile to a separation of the Germans of Austria from the Germans of the Reich. These pro-Reich tendencies within the old Austrian monarchy were embodied in the Pan-German movement led by Georg von Schönerer, which had its strongest roots in the Sudetenland. Schönerer's ideas deeply influenced Hitler. His movement was violently nationalist, anti-democratic, anti-liberal, anti-Austrian, anti-Catholic, anti-Semitic, and played about with the idea of the rebirth of the old German paganism; in fact, the whole Nazi programme. The defeat of Germany in the War discredited his ideas for a time, but on the other hand the nationalist feelings of the Germans in the Sudetenland were exacerbated since they had, through the peace treaties, come under Czech domination. When the economic slump of 1930 hit the Sudetenland even more severely than the Reich itself, and when a few years later the Nazis took the helm, the old Pan-Germanism re-emerged in full strength. No transition to Nazism was necessary because, in those regions, Pan-Germanism and Nazism were really one and the same thing.

Neither was there a need for a plebiscite in the Sudetenland. The municipal elections of May 1938 had shown all too clearly that the great majority of the population wanted to join Germany, not only because they were Germans, but because they were confirmed Nazis as well. The Sudetenland was the cradle of Nazism, and is its most faithful adherent today. Nazi Germany has acquired a thoroughly reliable population with the Sudetenland.

The cause of Austria is different. There Pan-Germanism had many converts before the War, but they had never been more than a minority. To the end the bulk of the population adhered to the Catholic and Socialist Parties. Since 1918, however, the little Austrian Republic, an artificial remnant of a larger empire, had lived in poverty and destitution. The peace treaties refused Austria the right to join the German republic, but among Socialist workers and Catholic peasants the idea of the *Anschluss,* of Austria joining Germany of her own free will, had taken deep root. In the Austrian Republic, in contrast to the Sudetenland, the desire to join the Reich extended far beyond the limits of the Pan-German movement.

It was a fearful ordeal for Austrians when joining Germany became identical with submitting to the Nazi regime. In the Sudetenland the advent of Nazism had given the pro-German movement a tremendous impulse. In Austria the consequences of this event were much more complex. The Socialists and a pro-German section of the Catholics departed from the ideals of the *Anschluss* as a result of the advent of the Nazis, and thousands who had previously wanted it now no longer wanted it. But there was Germany's rise to balance these effects, and then the depression hit Austria fearfully and made people see their only salvation in joining the Reich. As a result, the Nazis made deep inroads, especially among the peasant following of the Catholics. But their conquests were offset to an extent by their anti-Catholicism, which made at least the older generation of the peasantry hesitate to join their heretical ranks.

The result of all these trends and counter-trends was roughly this: in Styria, Carinthia, Vorarlberg, the Nazis had probably won a definite majority; in Salzburg, a narrow majority; in Tirol and in the Burgenland (the border region ceded to Austria by Hungary in 1921) about half; in Upper Austria a strong minority; in Vienna and Lower Austria a small minority.

The conquest of Austria in March 1938 has naturally changed the position. The Nazis had deeply undermined the strength of the Catholic Church in Austria, and the Episcopate with Cardinal Innitzer at its head immediately bowed to the conqueror and Heil-Hitlered the entering German troops. It can be confidently assumed that as a result resistance against the Nazis has broken down all over the countryside. A section of the Austrian peasants may be far less enthusiastic about Nazi rule than the Sudetenlanders but, after all, acquiesce in it. Vienna, with its dominating socialist movement, its old liberal tradition, and its high proportion of Jews, is different. It is the second city of the Reich; but it is difficult to see how it could ever be anything but disaffected.

The Sudetenland, therefore, became almost immediately an integral part of the Reich, whereas Austria presented difficulties. The independent Austrian army had to be dissolved; most of the higher officers and civil servants had to be replaced by men from the old Reich, and considerable resentment ensued. Few even of the old partisans of the Nazis in Austria were entrusted with positions of confidence. Austrians were regarded as unreliable. Austria today finds herself in a semi-colonial position, her natives systematically excluded from ruling their own country. The economic stresses soon to be mentioned added to the uneasiness created by these measures. It will not be an easy task for the Nazis to assimilate Austria.

This is the political position. How does the acquisition of these two regions affect the strength and the international position of the Reich? This can easily be gleaned from a list of the assets and liabilities acquired by the conquerors.

Strange to say, the biggest assets acquired by Germany are undoubtedly Austria's and the Sudetenland's unemployed. Both regions were distressed areas. The unemployment was larger than figures showed, because the various means tests reduced the figure of the statistically unemployed, and the available female labour and the young who had never seen work must be added to the whole. Austria and the Sudetenland together count roughly eleven million inhabitants. Something very near a million must have been immediately available for work. Now the presence of such a huge number of unemployed could not be regarded as an asset but rather as a heavy liability in a country with an unemployment problem. But unemployment is precisely the one economic evil from which Germany has been relieved by the Nazi regime. She is faced with an acute shortage of labour, and besides Italian, Dutch, Danish, and other workers, she imported considerable numbers of Austrians, even before 1938.

Austrian and Sudetenland workers are on the whole of highly skilled stock. A certain proportion of them have found and will still find work at home at their old trades, which are working again for the Greater German market after having been stopped by the depression. But a considerable number have been carried off for unskilled labour on roads, fortifications, etc., in the old Reich, under the German law for the compulsory conscription of labour. These workers, like those of the old Reich employed on these kinds of work, live under a sort of military discipline, while their families at home get only the scantiest allowances. There are flaws in the German achievement of overcoming unemployment. But undoubtedly the new supply of labour has helped the German Government to ease considerably the tension of the labour market.

Besides workers, the two newly acquired regions provide military recruits. The potential of German man power has been increased by about one-seventh. In the case of the Sudetenland, Germany will enjoy the additional advantage that the military reserves she has acquired are fully trained. Czecho-Slovakia, having been on the winning side in the Great War, was never disarmed, and in contrast to Germany and Austria had a conscripted army since 1918. Both Austria and the Sudetenland are able to provide troops naturally fitted for mountain warfare, which is rather a weak point in the German army. In the case of Austria, these advantages are somewhat offset by the fact that the officers' corps of the old Austrian army was on the whole strongly anti-German and had to be replaced by officers from the old Reich. Thus, while Germany acquires more men, her shortage of officers, already very serious, is becoming a still greater problem. Therefore the acquisition of the new territories is liable to delay for some little time the moment when Germany will be fully ready for war, the more so because both the Austrian and Sudetenland troops must be retrained with German methods and German material.

As to this material, there exists a great difference between Austria and the Sudetenland. The Austrian armament was regarded as worthless by the German staff and after the *Anschluss* was sold to Hungary down to the last button. The frontier fortifications of Czecho-Slovakia with their heavy guns and secret devices, however, are undoubtedly an important asset to Germany. It will be remembered how strongly Hitler, at Munich, insisted that no "installations" should be removed by the Czechs before the evacuation of the territory.

On the economic side, by far the most certain asset acquired by Germany was the conquest of the Austrian gold reserve equivalent to about $90,000,000. The enormous importance of this windfall is characteristic of the present German situation. Normally, the Austrian gold reserve would have been reasonably sufficient to cover the additional circulation of notes in Austria and would therefore not have brought any specific advantage to Germany. But Germany is living on an uncovered currency and on barter. She spent the Austrian gold reserve within less than a year on rearmament.

Here is one more characteristic aspect of the German trade situation as it has evolved during the last years. In 1935, the first year of German rearmament on a grand scale, the German trade balance had been seriously passive. But from that position Germany had recovered during 1936 and 1937, partly owing to her barter trade and partly owing to the boom which allowed her to export heavily to the free markets of the West. But in 1938 the trade balance was again heavily adverse to Germany. This was mostly due to the general recession in world trade, but also to such factors as the blacklisting of Germany in the United States, the boycott of German goods, deterioration in their quality and delay in their delivery owing to the overstrained state of German industry. The newly acquired territories, Austria and the Sudetenland themselves, contributed to the trade deficit, as we shall see in a moment.

In 1937 Germany had made a surplus of about 400,000,000 marks in her foreign trade. In 1938 this surplus had been transformed into a deficit of about the same amount. It is impossible to give these figures any meaning in terms of gold or sterling because no one knows what the mark is really worth. In her many barter and clearing agreements, Germany has been laying down separate exchange rates for every country and in most cases even different exchange rates for different types of transactions. These variations of the rate of exchange are a strong weapon in the hands of the German negotiators of trade agreements because they can manipulate the exchange rate at will. But it makes *valueless* any statistics which take the mark as a definite unit always of the same value. All we can say is that a German trade surplus has been converted into a heavy deficit. It is not easy to see how this deficit could again be converted into a surplus. Germany cannot get all she needs by barter agreements extremely favourable to herself. And given the speed of her rearmament, she must find it very difficult indeed to cover her requirements out of her exports, partly because there are no unlimited markets for her goods and partly because it is beyond her own resources to force rearmament at the pace she is doing and simultaneously force her export trade to the extent needed to cover her imports. Therefore German imports and exports can balance only in extraordinary years. In lean years she has simply no choice but to conquer foreign exchange in order to patch up the deficit. That Germany should be forced to expand in order to obtain foreign exchange may seem a fantastic position. It is nevertheless a reality, and a need for such expansion must inevitably recur within short intervals. Especially if, as in the case of Austria and Czecho-Slovakia, the new conquests are liable to add to the permanent deficit of her trade.

Here, as in so many other respects, German expansion only creates the need for still more expansion. That was very obvious in the case of the Sudetenland. There Germany hoped to get a new currency windfall, but her expectations did not materialize. She had expected to get part of the Czecho-Slovak gold reserve as cover for the Czech bank notes in circulation in the Sudetenland. But as Germany had refused in her turn to take over her share of the Czech debt, Czecho-Slovakia refused to give away her share of the gold reserve. Thus, in the case of the Sudetenland, Germany had burdened herself with new permanent needs to import without the compensation of a currency windfall. It was one of the main reasons for the march into Prague. She has now got control of the Czech gold reserve. But no windfall can still her gold-hunger for very long.

Why are Austria and the Sudetenland permanent burdens upon the German trade balance? The first answer to this query is simple: both were distressed areas though for different reasons. The little republic of Austria was a remnant of the old Habsburg monarchy, whose capital Vienna had lived on the resources of the whole empire. Once these resources were cut off, the two million inhabitants of Vienna were inevitably delivered over to misery. The Sudetenland, on the other hand, is a highly industrialized region, needing large markets. Some of these markets before the War had lain inside the Habsburg monarchy and had been lost by its disappearance. Others abroad had been severely hit by the world depression and by Japanese competition. The economic problems of the two areas are therefore rather different in kind. But they have certain features in common.

The trouble about them both, from the German point of view, is that they are markedly deficient in foodstuffs, which constitute a rather inelastic item of imports. Germany can deprive her Austrians and Sudetenlanders of butter and eggs, but not of bread. The Sudetenland has an additional serious deficiency of meat.

Both regions might pay for their deficiency of foodstuffs out of tourist traffic. The famous spas of Northern Bohemia and the Austrian mountain resorts have brought foreign currency to Austria and Czecho-Slovakia. But there is no doubt that the Nazi conquest has driven away a very considerable section of the custom of these places.

One additional factor of great importance is that the industry of both regions, and especially that of the Sudetenland, is now directly competing with the superior German industry in foreign markets. To cite one important instance, the Sudetenland cotton industry hitherto competed successfully with German goods in the U.S.A. market owing to the most-favoured nation clause which Czecho-Slovakia enjoyed while Germany was blacklisted in the American tariff. But since the Sudetenland has become German, Sudetenland goods are subjected to the same restrictions as German goods and their exports to the United States must heavily decline.

There are, unfortunately, few lines of production where the old Reich and the Sudetenland do not compete. Whether it is textiles, gloves, earthenware, toys, glassware, musical instruments or paper, Sudetenland goods always meet similar German goods on the market.

The situation could be slightly better in the case of Austria. A considerable section of her industry was turning out half-artistic goods with an appeal to special tastes. Austrian furniture, leather goods, etc., did not compete with German goods. But here the difficulty arises out of the German trade system. Those goods do not easily lend themselves to bartering in large quantities, and again exports are affected.

The industries of Austria and the Sudetenland now form part of a larger economic unit which should provide a larger market. But as industrialists in both regions always knew, there is no hope of their beating the producers of the old Reich with their superior technical outfit. Thus certain Austrian industries are declining. The Sudetenland industries keep their old markets in Czecho-Slovakia.

Moreover, in both Austria and the Sudetenland Germany has acquired certain raw materials she urgently needs. She is now self-sufficing in timber, controls almost all lignite (the raw material for artificial oil) available in Europe, and has acquired in Austria the largest European deposit of magnesite and an important amount of bauxite (the raw material for aluminum). With the acquisition of the Joachimsthal area in the Sudetenland she has come very near European monopoly in radium. Perhaps the most important gain is the acquisition of the Austrian iron-ore, though the 1,800,000 tons of annual Austrian production cover less than one-tenth of the German needs.

A clear distinction must be made between the value of these gains for the German trade balance and for the German war potential. All gains are important in relation to the trade balance, though here the assets must be offset against the liabilities. No figures are available to allow of any definite conclusion. But the heavy adversity of the German trade balance in 1938 proves that so far the newly acquired territories cannot really have helped Germany very much, and in the case of Austria it is almost certain that she is not only no help but a heavy burden.

Concerning the war potential, the situation is equally involved. The gains in the Sudetenland, primarily lignite and timber, represent a net advantage to Germany. The same could not be said of Austrian iron-ore, magnesite, bauxite, and timber because these were to a large extent available to Germany before the *Anschluss* and would in all probability have remained available in case of war. Here the advantage is limited to the saving of foreign exchange, whereas the direct effect on German military strength is nil.

It is not easy to sum up this very complex picture. The economic effects of the conquest of Austria and of the Sudetenland have probably been on the whole disadvantageous, the windfall of the Austrian gold reserve being overcompensated by a permanent burden upon the German trade balance. On the other hand Germany has temporarily relieved her labour shortage, slightly strengthened her supply of raw materials, considerably increased her strength in military man power, and slightly increased her supply in armaments. Against this stands as a serious factor the increased shortage of officers. Altogether it is not too favourable a balance, especially if one keeps in mind that with Vienna she has acquired a city second only to Berlin and clearly disaffected.

But we have not yet mentioned what is perhaps the most serious burden accruing to Germany by her conquests of 1938, that is, the tremendous expenditure involved in the task of reconstructing the newly acquired provinces. Railways and roads must be brought up to the German standard. The new army units must get German outfits. Those industries which can be made to work for military purposes must be modernized. All these may be minor charges upon a country living under normal conditions. To Germany with her overstrained industry and her serious shortage of raw materials it is a terrible task to face. This immediate liability diminishes the value of all the immediate assets gained by the conquest. This leads up to the problem which in the context of the Nazi regime must be the most important of all: What has been the effect of the tremendous successes of 1938 upon the German regime itself? Has it become more popular? Has it won increased prestige among the Germans themselves? Has it become more pacific or more aggressive?

The achievement of Greater Germany in itself ought to add enormously to the prestige of the regime. That such an old dream of the German people should materialize so suddenly and even without bloodshed ought to balance many sufferings Nazism has imposed upon the Germans. The regime ought to issue forth with greater strength from such an unequalled series of successes, and in consequence need not be so aggressive at home and abroad.

As a matter of fact, none of these natural consequences of the achievement of Greater Germany came about. Therefore the Munich agreement had almost immediately to be followed by a series of new German threats and aggressions. And at home, just after Munich, the Nazis reached the highest degree of horror they have so far achieved in the persecution of the Jews; also it is notorious that they are preparing a large-scale attack on the Christian churches. Since Munich, the frightfulness of the German regime has only increased.

The increased feeling of strength is partly responsible for this. But this is only one half of the story. The other half is that, strange as this may seem, mass feeling inside Germany has remained almost unaffected by the grandiose successes of Germany in 1938. Under normal conditions a regime which had succeeded on such a scale would be absolutely safe for one or even two generations. In Nazi Germany these successes have not been sufficient to allay for even a couple of weeks the deep psychological crisis through which the Nazi regime is passing at present.

This crisis has complex reasons. Some of them derive directly from the economic difficulties of the regime. Up to 1937, Nazism drew prestige from the gradual disappearance of unemployment, which offset the unchanging misery of starvation wages. But once the reservoir of the unemployed had disappeared, all subsequent economic changes were felt as changes for the worse: more work, worse food, worse supplies, worse disorganization of transport, worse labour conscription, worse taxation, more interference with the economic life of the individual. In the hectic atmosphere of Nazi Germany all these things constitute an intense strain and completely overshadow even the great successes in the international field. The constant rumble of the propaganda machinery makes things worse. It is not that propaganda has failed to foster certain attitudes in the German people. Most Germans, for instance, believed the stories about the atrocities allegedly committed by the Czechs against the Sudeten Germans. Yet the propaganda failed to have the expected psychological effect. People simply did not care about the supposed sufferings of the Sudeten Germans. They were sick of it all and especially of the idea that they should go to war to liberate their brothers across the border.

This fear of war is one of the most outstanding features of the present situation in Germany. Here the regime is in an impasse. For it has itself created that fear by its constant talk about the hostility of the whole world against the new Germany, about Jewish and Catholic world conspiracies against Nazism, about an alleged British policy of encirclement, and by its constant threats against its neighbours. Conscription, rearmament, the construction of fortifications at breathtaking speed, requisitions, and mobilizations bear out these fears. Hatred and fear of war are the predominant feeling among those German masses which Nazism set out to educate in a new spirit of heroism.

Here, as on so many other points, the obviously reasonable policy for a regime would seem a return to normalcy. But for all the reasons outlined above, the regime is unable to do this, though for a time propaganda may change its tune and talk peace instead of threats and aggression. In the end the regime will have to react against the psychological crisis with more and not with less aggression. It has already done so at home. Success in the international field is yielding rapidly decreasing results in terms of prestige at home. This is only one more reason why the regime will be driven to quite incalculable degrees of violence and aggression.

The final question, therefore, is: What, for Germany, was the importance of Austria and the Sudetenland in terms of further expansion? In itself, their conquest is of more than doubtful value for Germany. But as a step to further expansion the advantages gained by Germany are immeasurable. It is sufficient to say, in this respect, that Czecho-Slovakia, after Munich, was a broken reed. The Franco-Soviet alliance was broken. But more important than the breaking up of the French system of alliances in Eastern Europe is the defeat of Italy. Before 1938, Italy could regard Austria and Hungary as her dependencies. With Poland friendly to Hungary, and Czecho-Slovakia hostile to Germany, Italy had succeeded in creating a barrier against the German advance towards the South-East. With the conquest of Austria, the Germans broke that barrier. The immediate result was that Germany instead of Italy became the paramount power in the whole South-East. But this belongs to another chapter.

CHAPTER IV

POLAND AND LITHUANIA

WE now turn to the remaining claims which Germany may raise either on racial or on historical grounds for territory formerly belonging to the Reich. Let us begin with Germany's eastern border. Here, one German claim, the one for Memel, has already been achieved, despite Hitler's assurance before Munich that Germany had no further territorial demands. No less than four German claims against Poland are still unsettled. They concern the free city of Danzig, the Corridor, the province of Poznan (Posen), and Upper Silesia. Memel, of course, belonged not to Poland but to Lithuania. In reality, in spite of Lithuania's inveterate hostility towards Poland, the maintenance of Lithuanian rule in Memel was as much to Polish as to Lithuanian interest. In reality there are only two parties in the contest on the eastern border of Germany: Germany and Poland. The smaller Baltic countries are merely satellites. But behind the quarrel between Germany and Poland looms the greater antagonism between Germany and the Soviet Union.

From the advent of the Nazi regime down to the time of Munich, German territorial claims in the east were not very much in evidence, much less so, in fact, than under the Weimar Republic. This was due to the German-Polish non-aggression pact which Hitler concluded a few months after his advent to power. It was then his first big diplomatic success. The German Republic had never bowed to the decisions of the peace treaties concerning her eastern border, and when the Nazi regime came in, the Poles were particularly upset. Fearing to be the first victim of Nazi aggression, they sounded Paris about the possibility of a preventive war, but the suggestion was turned down. Marshal Pilsudski immediately effected a change of front and tried a policy of direct negotiation with Germany. Those were the months when the Stresa front, the bloc of Britain, France, and Italy against

Germany, and the Franco-Soviet pact, were in preparation. Hitler snatched eagerly at the opportunity of winning at least one friend.

Ever since, Polish policy, under the direction of Colonel Beck, Poland's Foreign Minister, has been very strongly pro-German. Disliking the idea of Russian support, and distrustful of the willingness of the western powers to help, Poland tried to keep friends with Germany. The Polish dictatorship both before and after the death of Marshal Pilsudski was only too grateful to have achieved a measure of security from abroad while fighting their many adversaries at home. And Hitler wanted to keep Poland quiet while conquering Austria and Czecho-Slovakia. Not only were German claims upon Polish territory left dormant, but Germany even avoided making claims on behalf of the seriously maltreated German minority in Poland. And in order not to offend Poland, Germany left Lithuania in possession of Memel.

All this suddenly changed after Munich. During the Munich crisis Poland had not entirely acted on Germany's whim and in the end had occupied more Czech territory than the Germans wished. The slice of Czech territory acquired by Poland is not large but it contains important coal mines and the supremely important railway junction of Bohumin. The only railway running from Berlin straight into Slovakia and towards the Black Sea passes through this place. Germany could never carry out a successful campaign in the Balkans or in the Ukraine without possessing Bohumin and its railway line.

But the question of Bohumin is of only secondary importance. If Germany after Munich suddenly changed her policy towards Poland it was simply due to the fact that she now regarded Poland as an easy victim. She launched a pincer movement against Poland from both north and south. In the south, the Carpatho-Ukraine was made a spring-board for the Ukrainian anti-Polish revolutionary movement. In the north, Germany threatened Lithuania through the conquest of Memel. The reaction against the double threat was the conclusion of the Polish-Soviet non-aggression pact and later on, after the occupation of Memel, the Polish demand for help from the west.

At that moment, the German-Polish situation in its kaleidoscopic transformation had already assumed a slightly different aspect. Germany, while occupying Bohemia, Moravia, and Slovakia, had had to leave the Carpatho-Ukraine to Hungary. The Hungarians there stamped out Ukrainian nationalism to the best of their ability, thus removing from Poland, for the time being, the threat of a Ukrainian rising. Germany certainly expects to recover control of the Carpatho-Ukraine later by gaining control of all Hungary. But in the meantime she had thrown the Ukrainians in the Carpatho-Ukraine to their worst enemies, and the effect of this German "betrayal" of the Ukrainian cause will not be forgotten by the Ukrainians. Even if Germany gains control of Hungary, now including the Carpatho-Ukraine, the Ukrainians are no longer very likely to rise at the bidding of Germany.

But at the same time, by acquiring Slovakia, Germany now threatens Poland directly from the south while her newly acquired influence in Lithuania threatens her from the north.

Memel's paramount importance for Lithuania was due to the fact that it was this country's only harbour. Out of this fact a terrible clash of interests arose. For there is no doubt that the Memellanders, almost to a man, wanted to go back to Germany. The wishes of the population of this small territory clashed irreparably with the vital interests of the country they belonged to. Whether two million Lithuanians should virtually lose their independence so that a hundred and fifty thousand Memellanders should be able to exert the right of self-determination is a problem beyond the power of human justice to decide.

The political structure of the little Memelland is very similar to that of the Sudetenland except that Memel before the War belonged to the Reich. The town and the surrounding country district have always been extremely conservative and this conservatism, with some help from inside the Reich, gradually transformed itself into Nazism. In the end all German representatives in the Diet of the Memelland were virtually Nazis.

The special situation of the Memelland was realized at the peace conference. As a compromise between German and Lithuanian claims, the area was taken from Germany but not given to Lithuania. Although Lithuania got free access to the sea, the territory remained under the administration of an inter-Allied commission. This lasted until, in January 1923, the Lithuanians took advantage of the growing tension between France and Germany preceding the French occupation of the Ruhr and occupied Memel by a *coup de main*. Following that, the Lithuanians made every effort to make the town and the territory Lithuanian, but without any appreciable success. The proportion of German to Lithuanian votes in the Diet remained steady at about five to one. Attempts to abolish the regional autonomy of the area failed. And resistance against Lithuania grew rather than declined.

This is the more surprising, because the greater part of the population of the countryside speaks not German but Lithuanian as its mother tongue. Only the town of Memel is completely German. The fact is that tens of thousands of Lithuanian-speaking peasants constantly voted German. For in these parts of the world religion is still more important than language. The Lithuanians of Lithuania proper are staunch Catholics, like the Poles. The Lithuanians of the Memelland are Protestants, like their German neighbours, and therefore feel German.

Economically, no German interests were affected by the Lithuanian possession of Memel. But as already stated, Lithuania was bound to become largely dependent on Germany by losing Memel. For about half her export of eggs and dairy products goes through Memel to England and could now be cut off by Germany any time she wished to do so. Domination of Lithuania, moreover, might lead to German domination of the other Baltic countries, Latvia, Estonia, and Finland, which are of great economic and strategic importance.

The acquisition of a hundred and fifty thousand more Germans is quite an insignificant gain for Germany. To acquire complete control of Lithuanian eggs and butter, products which Germany finds it very difficult to import, is certainly more valuable to her. But the decisive importance of Memel lies in the indirect results its acquisition by Germany may have upon the whole situation in the Baltic.

The whole position, therefore, is similar in many respects to that of the Sudetenland, though the problems are on a smaller scale. The German claims were justified by the undoubted and incontestable desires of the population. But the real importance of the claims lay not in their immediate effects but in their indirect consequences: in the case of the Sudetenland, the opening of the gates to the southeast; in the case of Memel, the opening of the gates to the Baltic. Here lies a significant difference between the growing German empire and older empires such as those of Britain and France. For Britain and for France the acquisition of valuable countries was at least one decisive aim of imperial expansion. But for Germany the regions she wants actually to make part of herself sometimes matter little. What she really desires is often not the increase of her territory but the expansion of her influence over territories which will formally remain independent. We shall meet that feature over and over again, and its full importance will only gradually emerge.

The antagonisms between Germany and Poland are of a different nature because in the Polish regions coveted by Germany the Germans are mostly a minority. The free city of Danzig (which is not Polish, but where Poland enjoys special privileges) is the only exception. She is thoroughly German, and for that reason was not given to Poland by the peace treaties but granted a sort of independence with special rights for Poland in the harbour. This compromise was devised for reasons similar to those applying in the case of Memel. For Danzig, the seaport at the mouth of the Vistula, was at the time Poland's only access to the sea.

Danzig never became Polish. But like the Lithuanians in Memel, so the Poles in Danzig attempted to make use of their special rights for Polonizing the city. As in the case of Memel, it was a complete failure.

The Nazis, however, found their job in Danzig much more difficult than in Memel. Danzig is a much bigger place, with a strong labour movement, and strongly Catholic. The presence of a League of Nations High Commissioner did not make the task easier. It needed a great deal of ruthless terrorism to destroy the opposition parties. But after years of struggle, the goal was reached, the Nazis became the only recognized party. The Gestapo took control of the Danzig police; the man power of the little country was quietly organized to make part of the German army in case of war; Danzig workers were exported to Germany; and Danzig wharfs got German armament orders. While all this happened, Germany carefully safeguarded Polish rights and interests so that no Polish interference disturbed the process of Nazification.

Today, Danzig for all practical purposes is part of the Reich save that Poland has certain rights in the harbour. In itself Danzig would have no positive value for Germany except its capacity to yield several thousands of workers and of army recruits. But its nuisance value in connexion with German-Polish politics is considerable. In possession of Danzig, Germany can always cut off Poland's water-borne export down the Vistula and the Baltic. Again, the indirect consequences of the Nazi conquest of Danzig are much more important than its immediate advantages to Germany.

But Poland has seen to it that this danger be reduced as much as possible. All through the history of the German Republic, the German Government tried to the best of its ability to create trouble between Danzig and Poland and so make it difficult for Poland to make full use of the Danzig harbour. As an answer to this policy, the Poles have constructed a harbour of their own in Gdynia (Gdingen), formerly a little fishing village on the small stretch of coast line on the Baltic owned directly by Poland. Gdynia is situated in the Polish Corridor, the Polish stretch of country cutting German East Prussia from the rest of the Reich since the peace treaties. Though the Corridor was granted to Poland expressly for the sake of giving Poland direct access to the Baltic, the Germans never believed that the Poles would be able to construct a harbour on that shallow and sandy beach.

They did, however, and connected it with the mining centres of Upper Silesia by direct railway built with French capital. Today, Gdynia takes about half of Poland's sea-borne export trade in weight and much more than half of it in value. Danzig could any day be ruined, as a harbour. And if it were closed to Polish transport, Poland could easily divert her whole trade from Danzig to Gdynia. Danzig has become relatively unimportant to both sides.

Gdynia and the Corridor, on the other hand, have only become all the more important. The Corridor constitutes the really tragic, insoluble problem between Germany and Poland. It is one of the many cases where one man's right is the other man's wrong. The Corridor is Poland's only access to the sea. And as it is equally impossible for her to export northward through Russia or Estonia or southward through Rumania and the Black Sea (because both routes would be much too costly) all her other practicable export routes at some point lead through Germany. Without the Corridor, Germany could subject Poland to virtual blockade.

On the other hand, as already said, the Corridor cuts right across German territory, dividing East Prussia from the rest of the Reich. Yet economically the Corridor is immeasurably more important to Poland than to Germany. Polish traffic through the Corridor to the coast is seven times the value of German traffic across the Corridor between East Prussia and the rest of the Reich. Germany enjoys special rights on the Corridor railways and the Polish transit tariffs are very reasonable. It is only since 1938 that Germany, owing to her extreme shortage of foreign exchange, found it difficult to pay for her transit.

Under the Weimar Republic, Germany complained that East Prussia, which was at any rate severely hit by the agrarian crisis, had lost markets in the Corridor and the province of Poznan. But whatever truth there was in these allegations, there is today no longer an agrarian crisis in Germany, which suffers not from a surplus but from a shortage of agricultural products. Today the agricultural surplus of the Corridor and of the province of Poznan would be valuable to Germany.

But from the German viewpoint the decisive objection to the Corridor is not economic but strategical. The Corridor is no serious obstacle to her trade. But it would be a serious obstacle to her military movements in case of war. If ever Germany attacked Russia, East Prussia would be one of her decisive bastions, and a hostile or even a neutral Poland could easily prevent her from moving a sufficient number of troops into that province. Germany therefore needs the Corridor if she wants to have a free hand for aggression in the East. And it is precisely the fact that Germany's possession of the Corridor would strangle Polish trade which makes the Corridor even more valuable for Germany. For only such a stranglehold could force Poland to give up her policy of balancing the Soviet Union against Germany and make her join on the German side. Again it is the indirect not the direct consequences of a possible German conquest that matter most. Whatever territory Germany may acquire from Poland is not so valuable in itself other than as a means of bringing Poland under control and gaining a starting point for an attack upon Russia.

On historical and linguistic grounds both sides can make valid claims to the contested terrritories. The Corridor (Western Prussia) belonged until 1466 to the Teutonic Knights, the precursors of modern Prussia; to Poland until the first partition of Poland in 1772, and again to Prussia until 1918. The province of Poznan was Polish until the second partition of Poland in 1793, changed hands repeatedly during the Napoleonic Wars, and finally became Prussian in 1815 and remained so until 1918. The Polish part of Upper Silesia was part of the Holy Roman Empire from the twelfth century and always remained under German rulers until 1918. It is the only section of Polish territory where historic rights speak clearly in favour of Germany. As to Poznan and the Corridor, only God Himself could decide whose historic right is to have precedence.

Unfortunately, the linguistic position does not in all cases agree with the historical one and is complicated by the occurrence of important changes since 1918. When the Republic of Poland was created in 1918, it contained about two million Germans (of a population

which numbered about thirty millions and which has since grown
to thirty-four). Of these, something less than half a million lived in
parts of Poland which had formerly been Austrian and Russian. Of
the remainder, no less than nine hundred thousand were squeezed
out by the Poles after the formation of the Polish State. German
officials, schoolteachers, etc., were summarily dismissed; German
workers could not find work; business men and farmers were ruined
by taxes and other methods of economic discrimination; and terror
was spread among the German minority by a campaign of unmoti-
vated arrests. The Germans, who are not very good at resisting pressure unless backed by official authority, put up hardly any fight and
left in a hurry. The exodus was much more considerable in the Corridor and in Poznan than in Upper Silesia. For the latter became
Polish only in 1922, after the first wave of Polish nationalism had
spent itself. When the League of Nations established the new border
as a result of the plebiscite, special safeguards were introduced in
favour of the German minority.

Before the disaster, the German minority in Poznan, and especially
in the Corridor, had been considerable. Today, in the two provinces
together, it has sunk to the insignificant figure of a little more than
three hundred thousand. But Germany need not recognize the present
state of affairs and may make a special grievance precisely of this
forced exodus and ask the return of the regions concerned.

As explained above, the area Germany really wants is the Corridor,
on strategical grounds. There would be good reasons for leaving Poznan alone, for this province has always been much more thoroughly
Polish in feeling than West Prussia and would be difficult for Germany to digest. Yet once Germany had acquired the Corridor, the
province of Poznan would stretch as a deep salient into German territory and (unless Germany had acquired firm control of the Polish
Government) might constitute a serious threat to Prussia proper.

The situation in Polish Upper Silesia is rather more favourable for
Germany than language statistics suggest. It is true that the majority
of the population speak Polish as their mother tongue, but a knowl-

edge of German is widespread and the population of the region has always been curiously indifferent to national issues. Before the War they felt Prussian and did not very much care which idiom they used. The coal basin of Upper Silesia is one of the most important industrial regions of Central Europe, and would be well worth having from the German point of view. Its importance has grown since Poland, after Munich, occupied the adjacent part of Czecho-Slovakia, belonging to the same coal basin and again with a considerable German minority. Moreover, one of the most important strategical railways of Europe runs through Bohumin, the railway junction recently acquired by Poland. It is the shortest route from Berlin to Budapest and to the Black Sea.

It remains to discuss the chances of Germany's carrying out her intentions concerning Poland. Germany finds herself confronted with a task which is anything but easy. The unpleasant peculiarity, from the German point of view, is that precisely those political forces which in other countries are apt to give in to German pressure are most ferociously hostile to Germany in Poland. There exists in Poland a party which calls itself National Democrats which may be everything Germany could wish for: wildly anti-Semitic, furiously anti-Bolshevik, anti-Russian, anti-socialist, anti-liberal, and full of what one generally calls Fascist tendencies. Compared with the National Democrats, the existing dictatorship, with its backbone in the army, is a relatively mild affair, however oppressive it may be. The ruling group in Poland is bitterly at odds with the National Democrats on their Right, while at the same time the regime is constantly threatened from the Left, the labour movement and the poor peasants, and in addition cannot fully master the resistance of the national minorities, Ukrainian, White Russian, and Lithuanian. In its weakness and instability, the Polish dictatorship, as represented by Colonel Beck, was until recently the group most inclined to come to an understanding with Germany.

But the masses are with the opposition of the Left and the Right, and the regime is much too weak to disregard their feelings. The Left is obviously strongly anti-German. But the peculiarity of the Polish situation is that the National Democrats, the party of the extreme Right, are the most anti-German of all. Their extreme nationalism originated in the fight against Prussian oppression before the War. Their leader Roman Dmowski is himself a native of Poznan, who all through his life has been ready to co-operate with anybody, whether the Tsar or the French Republic, in order to defeat Prussia. The National Democrats, ever since the beginning of the twentieth century, have held firm control of what are today the western provinces of Poland, just those provinces coveted by Germany. And their influence in these provinces is so great that the Government almost invariably chooses the governors of the western provinces from among their friends; these governors have fought the German minority even at times when this was not in agreement with the pro-German policy of the Polish Government. It is an irony of history that the German minority in Czech Silesia had good reason for bitter complaints when as a result of Munich they were transferred from Czecho-Slovakia to Poland. The first act of the Polish Governor was to dissolve all the German political organizations which had happily thriven in democratic Czecho-Slovakia.

Germany, therefore, should have little hope of breaking up Polish resistance from within. Poland is not Czecho-Slovakia. The Right in Czecho-Slovakia was constantly conspiring with Henlein against Beneš and his group. The Right in Poland could never play a similar role. For that reason Poland, in spite of all her weaknesses, would be a hard nut to crack. Yet cracked it must be, because without holding the Corridor and controlling Poland Germany can never really have a very strong position against the Soviet Union. And unless Germany achieves that, she cannot be sure of gaining and maintaining complete supremacy in the south-east. Here lies one of the most formidable problems of the future.

Here, too, lies the explanation of the German game with the Ukrainians. Germany can hardly hope to make much use of the rifts among the Poles. But she can hope to wear down Polish resistance through the minorities. There are about seven million Ukrainians in the south-east of Poland, two million White Russians in the east, about one million Lithuanians in the north-east, and something like a million Germans, mostly in the west; altogether about a third of the population of the whole republic. The hatred of the Ukrainians for the Poles is intense, and their strategic position most threatening. A revolt in the Polish Ukraine, backed from the Carpatho-Ukraine (the Ukrainian part of Czecho-Slovakia), would have taken Poland in the rear of its southern flank, whereas through East Prussia and a German-controlled Lithuania Germany might attack her in the north. Lithuania might be promised the return of Vilna, her old capital (snatched away by the Poles in 1920), in exchange for Memel. But the whole pincer movement is less of a threat to Poland just now, when Germany has allowed Hungary to occupy the Carpatho-Ukraine and to stamp out the local Ukrainian movement with fire and sword. It would not be a very threatening plan, at any rate, if either the Soviet Union or the western powers backed Poland. But there might be moments when help from either side would be equally unavailable. For such a moment Germany is obviously waiting. Until then she is playing at cat and mouse, alternately threatening and promising, alternately pushing the Ukrainians and the German minority forward and keeping them back. Whether she will succeed is another question. It is not very likely in view of the pledge recently extended to Poland by the British Government.

FINI

CHAPTER V

SLESVIG AND THE DOMINATION OF THE BALTIC

SMALL territorial gains can have tremendous indirect consequences. This applies emphatically to the German claims for North Slesvig.

Like the Corridor, Poznan, and Upper Silesia, so North Slesvig was lost to Germany by the peace treaties. Like these provinces, Germany claims her back from her new owner, in this case the helpless little kingdom of Denmark. As in the case of the territories ceded to Poland, the Germans form a small minority. But this minority has never been persecuted by the Danes as the German minorities in the east have been persecuted by the Poles.

Slesvig was under the Danish crown until the war between Denmark on the one side and Prussia and Austria on the other in 1864. After this war, the province remained under joint Austro-Prussian administration and was one of the bones of contention between the two countries which led to the war of 1866. Austria, after her defeat, left it to Prussia but stipulated that a plebiscite should be taken at a later date in the northern part of the province, where the majority spoke Danish. The pledge was never carried out, and first Austria, and much later Denmark, formally renounced the idea. But it was taken up by the Allies after the Great War, and a plebiscite took place after the peace treaty in two separate zones, the one with its centre in Flensburg, the other with its centre in Haderslev (Hadersleben). The Flensburg zone voted overwhelmingly German, the Haderslev zone overwhelmingly Danish. There were, however, several towns on the southern fringe of the Haderslev zone with a German majority. The result was not surprising, for it corresponded exactly to the results of ordinary pre-War elections. The Haderslev zone had invariably sent a Danish nationalist to the German Parliament.

After the transfer of the territory, German influence and German votes naturally declined still further owing to the withdrawal of

55

German officials. In the elections of 1935, the Germans in the area polled twelve thousand votes out of a total vote of eighty-one thousand; in those of 1939, fourteen thousand votes out of a total of ninety-six thousand. Germany's claims to North Slesvig are weak indeed, for nobody can seriously doubt the unobjectionable character of Danish elections.

The little area has no importance in itself whatsoever. It is mainly agricultural, and it is the peasant population which is mostly Danish, while German influence is stronger in the few small country towns. The acquisition of an area with an agricultural surplus might be welcome to Germany, but as the whole area has only a hundred and eighty-four thousand inhabitants, the advantage would be insignificant. The district has no particular strategic importance.

Yet there is no doubt that Germany covets it. Or more exactly here, as in so many other places, Germany is playing at cat and mouse. Time and again the German foreign office has disclaimed any designs upon North Slesvig. But the local rulers on the border, in Kiel and in Flensburg, act in a different manner. Quite officially they organize a Nazi Party, Storm Troops and all, in North Slesvig, that keeps close watch over the German minority and puts forward thinly veiled demands for a return of the area to Germany. A big Nazi meeting in April 1938, after the fall of Austria, launched the slogan, "The swastika must wave as far as the Kongeaa" (the pre-War boundary river between Germany and Denmark).

As North Slesvig is neither German-speaking nor valuable in itself, these claims can only aim at some other goal. And it is not difficult to discern that again the territorial demands are merely a cover for the real aim—that of establishing a firm control over a formerly independent country. Germany keeps the claim for North Slesvig up her sleeve in order to break Denmark.

If North Slesvig is unimportant, Denmark is not. Though only a small country with three and a half million inhabitants, she is, next to New Zealand, the best world producer of dairy products. And dairies are one of the weakest spots in the German system of supplies. Yet

Danish dairies in themselves would not be a sufficient reason for political action on a grand scale. But as Slesvig is only a means of access to Denmark, so Denmark herself is only an access to larger spheres. She dominates the entry to the Baltic. She is a natural bridge between Germany and the Scandinavian mainland. The control of Denmark is one of two keys to the control of the whole Baltic area in case of war. The other key is the Åland Islands in the northern part of the Baltic, which are Finnish and about which we shall say something in a moment.

Firm control of the Baltic is one of the most vital of German interests. Swedish iron-ore is the most vital of all raw materials for German armament, and Germany, in case of war, would have to accept any risks whatsoever in order to secure continuous supplies. Denmark, Lithuania, and Latvia are important as a means of supplying Germany with food and that under conditions where Germany will have no money available to pay for it. Latvia, Estonia, Finland, and Sweden have rich supplies of timber.

Yet the strategic and political importance of the Baltic is even greater than its economic one. The Baltic (and the land route across Finland, Sweden, and Norway) is the nearest out of three possible communications between the Soviet Union and the West; the other two being through the Polar Sea and through the Dardanelles. The value of the Arctic route is very limited. The other two routes Germany threatens to cut. The Danish Sund and the Dardanelles have always been crossroads of world history.

All sorts of economic and political drives are inseparably intermingled in the German advance in the Baltic. Political action is made subservient to Germany's economic ends, and German economic influence in its turn helps to strengthen her political penetration. Yet the difficulties Germany meets in the Baltic are great indeed. They are of different kinds in two different groups of countries.

Denmark, Sweden, and Norway are democracies, all three for many years under Socialist Governments which enjoy tremendous popularity. Lithuania, Latvia, and Estonia are dictatorships and could therefore be more amenable to German political views. And in Latvia and Estonia, before the War, the Baltic lords of German stock and language had been the hated rulers over an exploited native peasantry. The liberation of these regions was marked by the expropriation of the German landlords, and deep distrust of Germany is engrained in the soul of every Latvian and Estonian.

Finland is a case of transition between the two groups. It has seen serious attempts to create a dictatorship and is not quite so democratic as the Scandinavian countries. Then, too, Finland never knew the Germans as enemies. On the contrary, in 1918 the Germans helped in the liberation of Finland from Russian domination and from Bolshevism. The best chances for Germany seem therefore to lie in Finland, and this is important owing to the strategic role of the Åland Islands. But of late the strength of the extreme Right in Finland has much declined, and Finland has drawn closer to the Scandinavian countries. Its Government, too, is now under preponderant Socialist influence.

A common feature of all Baltic countries is their dislike of Russia and their strong sympathy for Britain. Britain and Germany between them take by far the greatest share of Baltic trade and strongly compete for Baltic markets. The seven Scandinavian and Baltic countries receive no less than twelve per cent of all British exports. And in every single one of these countries British political ideals are competing with German ones. The Baltic is an important zone of conflict between German and British interests.

Commercial and political trends have been somewhat contradictory. Britain in this region has just held her own commercially, while the importance of German trade has been steadily growing. But with the growth of German aggressiveness, the political feelings and sympathies of all the Baltic countries, both democracies and dictatorships, turn more and more towards Britain.

German pressure is the most severe in Denmark. One of its levers is the Nazi movement in North Slesvig and among the Danes themselves. German trade policy is another, and its effects are the stronger because Denmark and especially Danish agriculture have been severely hit by the depression and by the Ottawa agreements. The heavily indebted Danish farmers need markets desperately, and Germany offers markets, if not for Danish bacon, butter, and eggs, at least for Danish cattle. But in exchange, Germany, which has a free hand to buy cattle elsewhere, has forced extremely unfavourable conditions upon Denmark. The commercial agreement of 1936 between Germany and Denmark obliges Denmark to accept, in clearing against exports to Germany, textiles, machinery, and other goods which are being increasingly produced by the growing Danish industry itself, and this is only one of the many unpleasant features of this trade agreement. So unfavourable indeed is it that it has been constantly rumoured that in part this trade agreement is the price paid by the Socialist Danish Government for the temporary maintenance of North Slesvig under Danish rule.

One of the results is that the unemployment figures in Denmark remain at a very high level. It is the only Scandinavian country which has not really recovered from the depression. Thus unemployment is gradually sapping the strength of the labour movement while the peasants look eagerly towards Germany for increased exports and would be prepared to remove any grievances Germany might raise. The political effects of this situation are not negligible, though there are a number of obstacles which make it difficult for Germany to remove rapidly the existing Left Government. The Danish upper classes, and especially the Conservatives, the party of the Copenhagen bourgeoisie, are traditionally anti-German since the War of 1866, as indeed are the Danish people as a whole. Attempts to form a Danish Fascist party on Nazi lines have so far met with limited success only; the election of April 1939 for the first time gave the Danish Nazis three seats in the chamber. The peasant party so far still holds out the best hopes for a peaceful German penetration and Danish peasant organizations have been the only Scandinavian organizations of any real importance which have so far responded to invitations to Nazi rallies in Germany.

Yet Denmark is a country so weak that Germany could control her by means of direct threats without much help from within. Already during the Great War it was stated that hardly anything could be done against a German attack upon Denmark, and today this holds good all the more, since in her desperately exposed situation Denmark has preferred to emphasize rather than to cure her weakness. She is the only country in Europe which has not rearmed to any great extent and lies open to an aggressor.

Germany makes use of this position to exert pressure of a special kind which she attempts to exert in many countries, but nowhere so successfully as in the case of Denmark. She threatens vague evils if anything anti-German is printed in the Danish press. In the case of Denmark this goes to incredible lengths. *Berlingske Tidende,* the largest Danish newspaper, reprinted, not news about Germany, but the debate in the British House of Commons after Munich with the unfavourable comments made by certain members upon German terrorism against anti-Nazis in the Sudetenland. This quotation was made the object of a diplomatic action on the part of Germany and the foreign editor of *Berlingske Tidende* had in fact to go—an event probably unique in the history of diplomatic relations. Similar pressure with similar success has been exerted upon the Government paper, *Social-Demokraten.*

Thus, in effect, nothing very anti-German can be printed in Denmark. It may be contended that the Danish press remains free to discuss Denmark's home affairs. But in a quiet little country such as Denmark home news is not very exciting and the real alinement of forces takes place with regard to international affiliations. The Danish press may print anything anti-Russian or anti-British but nothing anti-German. Already, though in a covert form, a German press censorship is at work in Denmark. It is a decisive step in the establishment of Nazi totalitarianism.

In spite of economic difficulties and of threats from the south, democratic, anti-German, and pro-British tendencies are too strongly rooted in Denmark to be easily upset. Yet this is how the diplomatic correspondent of the *Sunday Times* [London] summed up the situation:

"The small German minority is highly organized from within the Reich, and the German legation in Copenhagen has active contacts with every section of the Danish people. This is gradually leading to a general weakening of belief in the vigour of democracy, particularly as it is felt that Great Britain does not show herself interested in Denmark and makes no effort to counteract the German anti-democratic propaganda. Keen observers are thus beginning to wonder whether under these conditions democracy will survive in Scandinavia, and in Denmark there are already the beginnings of a Danish Nazi Party."

Sweden is different, for many reasons. She has no German minority within her borders. She has no common land boundary with Germany, and as long as Denmark remains independent could only be attacked by sea. She has seriously rearmed and is prepared to fight. Her Socialist Government is in close co-operation with the peasants, and there exists no great chance of a rift between workers and peasants concerning the attitude to take as against Germany. Furthermore, Sweden is at present exceedingly prosperous and has succeeded in swallowing up almost entirely the army of unemployed which was her nightmare during the fifteen years after the War.

The decisive fact is that Germany needs Sweden much more than Sweden needs Germany. Swedish iron-ore, covering about two-fifths of Germany's present needs, is absolutely indispensable for German rearmament. It is German rearmament which to a large extent has produced the boom in Sweden and incidentally strengthened the position of the Socialist Government there. Of this the Swedish Socialists are not unaware. All Swedish iron mines are either State-owned or State-controlled, and the Government might refuse Germany the iron she needs. But nothing of the sort has ever been tried. Seventy-five per cent of the Swedish exports of iron go to Germany.

Normally, big German imports from a country make it more dependent on Germany. But in this case Germany cannot use her imports as a weapon. For in this era of rearmament Sweden could easily place most of her exports elsewhere, whereas Germany has no free choice. Under these conditions the Germans are treading their way very carefully. The German press systematically refrains from attacks upon the Socialist Government in Sweden, emphasizes the racial affinity between Germans and Swedes (but these pure Nordics are not particularly interested), and altogether avoids giving offence.

Yet the Swedes are well aware that this situation cannot last. In the event of a serious international conflict, the land route through Sweden from Russia to the Atlantic, and Swedish iron-ore, would become all-important. Besides, Sweden is just one of those smaller industrial countries which Germany might be glad to fit into her economic system to provide her agricultural vassals in the south-east with industrial goods. Swedish policy is cautious but preparing for the worst. The crucial point in these preparations is the fortification of the Åland Islands, which concerns Finland even more than Sweden.

Finland is economically much less important to Germany than Sweden is, but strategically even more. Through Finland, Russia can be attacked directly. The Finnish Right, as already mentioned, has always been strongly pro-German since the German intervention on their behalf in the War against the Reds in 1918. And Nazi Germany ought easily to be able to get control of Finland by bringing to the helm a party entirely subservient to its aims.

But if there is any country where Germany has overplayed her game, it is Finland. She put too much hope upon the anti-Russian, anti-Communist, and anti-democratic Lapua movement of reactionary peasants, Lutheran clergymen, and retired officers of the "White" army of 1918. This movement came to the brink of complete success in 1932, at the pit of the depression, but declined with recovery, after having realized its chief official aim, the dissolution of the Communist Party. Since then, the extreme wing of the movement has become much more truculent and must today be regarded as completely Nazi. But precisely owing to this development, the movement, which at one time had been almost representative of the whole Finnish Right, split; the greater part of the Right went back to constitutionalism, and at present Finnish Fascism is insignificant. Whether it would remain so in a new depression is a different question.

At any rate, the movement had identified itself too much with Nazism for Germany not to feel the after-effects. When in 1935 the last attempt at a *coup d'état* collapsed miserably without bloodshed, a strong reaction in favour of Britain and democracy was the result. It brought to the head the present coalition Government under Socialist leadership. And this political development has so far not been seriously upset by the undoubted headway German trade has made in Finland as against the established position of Britain.

The effects of all this upon Finnish foreign policy have been considerable. In 1935, when Germany believed herself very near to getting control over Finland, she peremptorily asked her to fortify the Åland Islands so that in case of war Russia's Baltic fleet should be blocked in Kronstadt. The demand was incompatible with a treaty of 1920 between Sweden and Finland which had given the islands to Finland (more or less against the will of their inhabitants), but on condition that they should never be fortified; for the Åland Islands lie not only across the gateway from Leningrad into the Baltic, they lie directly opposite Stockholm as well. Finland kept this treaty faithfully and rejected the German demands.

But two years later she changed her mind under growing German pressure and decided to seek the consent of Sweden for the fortification of the islands, which was readily granted. The island group has since been strongly fortified, not against a possible attack from Russia but from Germany. The strategic position of the islands is exceedingly strong, and Sweden and Finland have seen to it that no German landing corps should be able to strike unexpectedly at the iron mines of central and northern Sweden or at Russia across Finnish territory.

No wonder that Germany was angry and tried a counter-coup. Mr. Holsti, the Finnish Foreign Minister who had concluded that agreement, was known to be a staunch democrat and an anglophile. His personal position in the cabinet was not a strong one, for reasons which had little to do with his attitude to international affairs. The Germans snatched at the opportunity of some rather strong anti-German utterances of his in the days of the Munich crisis, and a German protest brought him down. But again, Germany had miscalculated. His successor is certainly not any more pro-German than he was himself.

To round off the picture, a word must be said about German relations with Latvia. (Relations with Estonia are friendly but not very important.) In Latvia the Germans are constantly raising the grievances of the strong German minority which, like all minorities in Latvia, is treated with scant consideration. But in Latvia this is a dangerous game. There are other countries, such as Rumania and Brazil, where the German minority is popular and can easily be used as a spearhead for German penetration. In Latvia, where national liberation and the breaking of the influence of the Baltic barons were almost one and the same thing, the situation is different. German papers complain bitterly about the lack of understanding of Germany in Riga. But now, since the capture of Memel and the capitulation of Lithuania, Latvia may at any time be threatened with the use of main force.

Thus, in the whole Baltic area, Denmark is, so far, the only country where Germany has had definite success, though of a limited kind. Yet Denmark is the gateway to the rest, and Germany is making every conceivable effort to get control of the whole region, as she must. A German Empire without complete control of the Baltic is as unimaginable as a German Empire without complete control of the Balkans. If the latter has got so much more attention than the former, it is only due to the fact that the Nazis have been more successful so far in the south-east than in the north.

CHAPTER VI

THE NETHERLANDS, BELGIUM, FRANCE, SWITZERLAND, TIROL

Continuing our list of German territorial claims, and their direct and indirect implications, we are brought to her western borders. It is the zone where at present German intentions are least conspicuous. In the east and in the north, Germany is surrounded by small countries, some of them of recent origin and little stability, which are an easy prey to aggression. But across her western border Germany finds in France a first-rate military power which it is not so easy to deal with. The Netherlands and Belgium, which in themselves are helpless enough, cannot be touched without rousing against Germany all traditional feelings of Britain about the independence of these countries. Switzerland, whose strategic position between Germany and Italy is particularly unfavourable, can yet, to a considerably degree, rely on French support. Any German aggression in the west or south-west is bound to produce an international crisis much more serious than that of Munich and which in the present state of things would almost certainly be bound to lead to war. As long as the Anglo-French alliance holds firm, Germany therefore will operate with great caution in this region.

Yet Germany's ultimate territorial claims in this area are perhaps bigger than in any other one. Two-thirds of the population of Switzerland speak German. They are divided from Germany by a history of their own and a profoundly different mentality, yet Germany is almost openly working for the acquisition of the German-speaking part of Switzerland in the future. In the north the Dutch, and the Flemish in Belgium, speak languages of their own, but these languages are linguistically much nearer to German than the Scandinavian languages and are really only Low German dialects which have evolved into literary languages. German nationalists have never recog-

65

nized the Dutch and Flemish as individual nationalities and always regarded them as lost tribes of the original stock which ought to be brought home to the motherland. During the Great War, a serious attempt in that direction was made in the Flemish-speaking part of Belgium. Today, when Dutch neutrality, in case of war, is less assured than ever, the Dutch are rightly afraid of the same fate. Finally, there is German-speaking Alsace, of which more later.

If Germany has so far kept up a certain reserve in voicing her aims in these parts of the world, it does not mean that she has not made progress. On the contrary, and perhaps precisely owing to her reserve, she has brought about, in the west, one of the most brilliant strokes of her international policy. She has succeeded in loosening the close ties which linked Belgium with France and Britain.

The territory lost by Germany to Belgium as a consequence of the war is insignificant. It is the little zone of Eupen-Malmédy, with about seventy thousand inhabitants. The economic value of this district is negligible. Part of the region is very poor. There are, however, a few zinc mines. Malmédy always spoke French and is loyal to Belgium. Eupen always spoke German, and before the advent of the Nazis was not very pro-Belgian. But since 1933 the Catholic element in the district prefers Belgium to Germany, and in the elections of October 1938 nearly half of the vote in the city of Eupen went against the Nazis. The countryside is politically more or less indifferent.

In the peace treaty the region was handed over to Belgium without asking the opinion of the population. Afterwards, a strange procedure, quite inappropriately called a plebiscite, was carried out. Lists were opened after the territory had become Belgian, and people were allowed to sign them as a protest against the annexation. This extremely unfair procedure of an open vote, after the *fait accompli* of annexation, was made worse by a great deal of administrative chicanery. Germany's case really rests on the inadequacy of this so-called plebiscite. Belgium has repeatedly considered returning the district of Eupen to Germany, and even today there certainly exists a case for a local plebiscite under fair conditions. It might long ago have been taken were it not certain that such a plebiscite would create a dangerous precedent for other German claims, much less justified in themselves.

The characteristic thing about Eupen-Malmédy, however, is that here, in contrast to North Slesvig, the Nazis have not pressed their claims to any extent. A quarrel about this unimportant region would only rouse suspicions in Belgium, and Belgium, in contrast to Denmark, is willing to defend herself. Germany has much more efficient means of winning a footing in Belgium, and her tactics would only be upset by raising untimely territorial demands.

Two factors of the greatest importance work for Germany inside Belgium. The one is the undoubted crisis of Belgian democracy. The other is the fight between the Flemish and the Walloons, whose literary language is French.

The crisis of Belgian democracy is due to the inadequacy of the Belgian political machinery to the difficult economic tasks now facing a country living primarily on exports. There are three traditional parties in Belgium—Socialist, Catholic, and Liberal—and none of them is ever strong enough to form a government of its own. Moreover, all three parties are divided within themselves on national lines; the Liberals less than the other two, but then they are the weakest party. The Catholics are divided in addition between a very reactionary Right Wing controlled by the landed aristocracy and a strongly progressive Left Wing controlled by the Catholic trade unions. The Catholic Party, which is traditionally the strongest party in the country, can hardly be regarded as a political unit at all. Every attempt on the part of the Catholics to form a one-sided coalition either with the Socialists or with the Liberals threatens a split within the party. But without Catholic participation no majority is normally to be had. For many years, therefore, the country has been ruled by coalitions of all three traditional parties. The binding together of such contradictory forces naturally tends to create recurrent political stalemates, frequent Government crises, and a general feeling of uneasiness, made worse by the absence of any regular parliamentary opposition.

It was not surprising, therefore, that as an aftermath of the depression, and during the very slow recovery following it, a real Fascist movement grew in Belgium under the leadership of one Léon Degrelle. This movement, called the "Rexists," was at one time very dangerous, but during the last few years, with full recovery, it has disintegrated and finally relapsed into insignificance at the municipal elections of April 1939. This disintegration of Fascist movements (outside Germany and Italy) which sprang up during the depression is not limited to Belgium. We have already met a parallel case in Finland, and we shall soon meet a few more. Yet it must not be forgotten that the Nazis themselves, in Germany, collapsed after the recovery of 1924, only to re-emerge victoriously with the next depression.

The Rexists have most of their following in the French-speaking part of the country, which ought to make them anti-German. But it does not. The common ideology is stronger than the national antagonism, and the Rexists must on the whole be accounted a pro-German force.

The same applies, surprising though it is, to the extreme conservative wing of the Catholic Party. The Belgian Catholic aristocracy does not feel itself either French or Flemish. It was horrified by the Popular Front Government in France and by the Spanish Civil War, which it interpreted as threats of international revolution. Thus, even among the French-speaking section of the Belgian population, Germany has friends.

But the Flemish movement is a much stronger asset for the German game in Belgium. For centuries the Flemish have been treated as a sort of inferior race by the French. They gradually emerged to national consciousness in the eighties and ever since the Flemish national movement has made steady progress.

The Flemish actually are a slight majority of the Belgian population, and this majority is bound to grow for a long time because the Flemish birth-rate is higher than that of the French. The political significance of this situation came to the surface gradually as the Flemish became increasingly conscious of their nationality and the Flemish national movement permeated all political parties. For a long time the Flemish strove for equality. Today they strive for domination, and it is the Walloons who are creating defence organizations against the rising Flemish flood. During recent years every cabinet crisis has ended in an increase of Flemish influence until the Flemish had a clear majority in the cabinet.

Every political view is represented in the Flemish nationalist movement. The Flemish are a strong and influential minority in the Socialist Party. They actually control the Catholic Party. And they have a number of smaller nationalist parties proper, of whom some at least are openly Fascist, anti-Belgian, and pro-German. But in reality pro-Germanism is general in all sections of the Flemish national movement. The strength of this feeling can be gleaned from the fact that the Socialist Burgomaster of Antwerp, Camille Huysmans, former general secretary of the Socialist and Labour International, in 1937 went to the Cologne International Fair and there made an exceedingly pro-German speech, emphasizing the deep sympathy of his city for Germany and her achievements and the need of close co-operation between the two countries. It was an action which could not have any parallel among, say, Scandinavian Socialists.

But even the most extreme sections of the Flemish are only pro-German. They do not share the Nazi view that the Flemish are really Germans. Yet this view is diplomatically suppressed in Germany, and in the meantime Germany, in Belgium, is in the agreeable position of enjoying the full support of a non-German nationalist movement. At the present juncture this movement is not revolutionary in any proper sense. But it is full of revolutionary implications. It would be easy for Germany, with its help, to split Belgium in two in a serious crisis. It would be easy for her to strengthen the separatist wing in the Flemish movement, and to support the ideas of those of the Flemish who want to create a Greater Netherlands out of Flanders, the Netherlands, and South Africa. In a big international crisis, the Flemish nationalist movement might easily be used for permeating the Netherlands with Fascist ideas.

But just as easily Germany can use the Flemish for bringing Belgium as a whole under their control. At the present juncture the pro-German elements already dominate the Catholic Party, where both the Flemish and the Conservatives are pro-German. With the support of the Flemish Fascists, the Flemish wing of the Socialists, and the Rexists, they could easily overcome the resistance of the French section of the Socialists, the Liberals, and the small anti-German section of the Catholic Party.

These are only trends; they are not inevitable developments. The various groups just mentioned have only their pro-Germanism in common. Otherwise they are bitterly hostile to one another. Sections of the Flemish movement may turn round when they realize the extent of German ambitions, and a very great deal depends on both the economic and the international situation. Yet this much is certain, that at least half of the Belgian population today would be very reluctant to fight against Germany and would probably be ready to fight for it. As a result of this, the Belgian alliance with France was denounced in 1936, and there is no telling how far things will go once the crisis of Belgian democracy deepens. That Belgium of all countries should prove so very permeable to Nazi influence must be regarded as an extraordinary achievement and a serious threat to the vital interests both of Britain and of France. Besides, it would be a natural aim for German economic policy to draw Belgium with her big industrial plant into the orbit of the German economic system.

Farther north, in the Netherlands, Germany has been much less successful, because conditions there are much less propitious. There does not exist in the Netherlands a national grievance such as the Flemish question in Belgium. Dutch democracy is working smoothly. The very strong Calvinist and sectarian tradition of the country is incompatible with Nazism. Dislike of Germany is traditional and fairly general. So far the Nazis could obtain nothing in the Netherlands except the formation of a Dutch Nazi Party, which at one time seemed to have good prospects but which collapsed at the last parliamentary elections. Here again an unfavourable development of the economic situation might threaten a change. But at present the situation in the Netherlands is much more similar to that of Denmark than to that of Belgium. Nazi permeation is insignificant, but the country lives in constant fear of direct German conquest, which it would be very difficult to ward off. In the meantime every German handbook of geography insists upon the decisive importance for Germany to control the mouth of the Rhine.

On the southern end of the Franco-German border, in Switzerland, the situation is again very different. There the Germans hide their ultimate aims much less than in Belgium and the Netherlands. They do not limit themselves to supporting a local Swiss Fascism, fighting for the creation of a totalitarian regime in Switzerland. They go further and organize and finance a German Nazi movement in Switzerland which stands for a sort of *Anschluss* of German Switzerland to Germany. A constant series of conflicts between Germany and the Swiss Government has arisen out of this situation. One day it is the question of a certain newspaper such as the *Schweizer-Degen,* openly proclaiming the whole Nazi programme and slinging mud at all Swiss political institutions and political men, until the Government finds itself obliged to suppress the publication. Next it is a referendum in the canton of Basel for the suppression of the Nazi Party which calls forth a German diplomatic protest. Then Swiss public opinion is roused by the fact that a German attaché, who in Prague controlled the Henlein movement, is transferred to Bern, where he is suspected of being entrusted with a similar task. Then again, an incident is created by the discovery that the German Government is systematically sending German students to Swiss universities under the pretence of study but in reality for purposes of political propaganda.

The most serious conflicts, so far, have arisen over the liberty of the Swiss press. Germany is following her policy of suppressing all anti-German comment abroad with particular insistence in Switzerland, maintaining that every word of anti-German criticism is incompatible with Swiss neutrality. They have insisted on the suppression by the Federal Council of an international paper under Communist influence at Geneva, *Le Journal des Nations*. It was a sort of compensation for the suppression of Nazi papers. But on the whole, German pressure in that direction has been less successful in Switzerland than in Denmark. Altogether, Germany cannot boast much success in her dealings with Switzerland. The Swiss are a conservative people and in the beginning certain features of the German regime were attractive to a not inconsiderable section of the population. But then there are three things the Swiss care for above everything: their independence, their free institutions, and the unity of their three (or, more precisely, four) nationalities within one country. German propaganda for an *Anschluss* of German Switzerland has aroused apprehensions about all three points and in consequence has driven the unexcitable and slow-moving Swiss to a pitch of anger, fear, and indignation. Today extensive military preparations are being carried out in Switzerland, and no secret is made of their object: they are directed against a possible German attack upon Switzerland.

Switzerland has this in common with Sweden, the Netherlands, and Belgium, that it is one of the smaller industrial countries neighbouring on Germany which could be fitted with relative ease into the German economic structure. Moreover, like the other three countries just mentioned it is a capital-exporting country. And as in the political so in the economic sphere Germany has been more outspoken in her aims in Switzerland than in Belgium, the Netherlands, and Sweden. After Munich, an article in the *Deutsche Volkswirt,* semi-official organ of the German Ministry of Economics, tersely suggested that since Germany was now master of the South-East, Switzerland would be well advised to fit her economic system closely into that of Germany, unless she wanted to lose her financial and export assets in that part of the world. Such outspokenness was characteristic of the first few weeks after Munich. On the Swiss side it was easy to point out that Germany might be interested in diverting Swiss export trade from France to the Balkans, but that no paramount Swiss interests were involved in that area. Also, during the following month it became obvious that the German hold on the Balkans was less secure than was at first believed. Germany thus lacked all means of economic pressure upon Switzerland, and the only result of this feeler was to arouse indignation in Switzerland. The importance of the incident lies in the fact that here for the first time the German need for the control of further industrial regions was openly proclaimed.

In 1935 Germany acquired the Saar and in 1938 the Sudetenland. She hopes to acquire Polish Upper Silesia and German Switzerland. If Sweden, Belgium, and the Netherlands were added to them as economic zones of influence, it would mean an enormous strengthening of the German industrial potential. But it's a long way to that goal.

Switzerland is very important, too, in connexion with the Rome-Berlin Axis. During the abortive crisis of January-February 1939 it became apparent that Germany, in case of war, would try to support Italy with troops in Africa. At present the Axis has at its disposal only two railway lines, the one across the Brenner and the other (running very near the Yugoslav border) from Salzburg through Carinthia. In case of war, these two railway lines might easily become congested and form, as it were, a bottleneck. For full-fledged German-Italian co-operation in war the Gotthard railway, running across Switzerland, is probably indispensable. This need squares well with the Italian desire (dating back long before the Great War) of acquiring the Italian-speaking Swiss canton of Ticino, through which the southern branch of the Gotthard railway runs.

Let us finally emphasize that politically the case of Switzerland is entirely different from that of, say, Denmark. In Scandinavia, Germany cannot wish to acquire anything but indirect control and political domination. German Switzerland Germany wants to annex, as she annexed Austria and the Sudetenland. It is this desire for annexa-

tion which stirs such indignation among the Swiss. Here German
politics has fallen victim to German national superstitions. It is on
the grounds of common language that the Germans imagine that
Switzerland must become German. (They are musing on similar
intentions for similar reasons in the case of Flanders and the Netherlands.) But in fact language, strong tie though it is today, is not
everything. And the Swiss, with their factual independence dating
back to the fourteenth century, and their deeply engrained liberal
traditions, feel that in the political sense of the word they are emphatically not Germans. Germany might conquer Switzerland by force,
but she would only acquire a territory much more thoroughly disaffected than even Vienna.

Important as the Netherlands, Belgium, and Switzerland are in
themselves, the indirect results of a possible German control of these
countries are again more important than the direct ones. In the case
of the Netherlands and Belgium, their chief importance lies in the
threat against Britain which could be exerted from their coast. German politics both in Belgium and in Switzerland aims at the en-
circling of France. The latter obviously is a major goal of German
policy. The destruction of French power has been proclaimed in *Mein
Kampf* as one chief aim of Germany policy. The superficial *rapprochement* between Germany and France after Munich ought not
to foster the idea that Germany has renounced that aim. On the contrary, every move of German policy has been in that direction. At
Munich, Germany wrecked France's best ally in Europe. At the same
time she wrecked the Little Entente, the alliance between Czechs,
Rumanians, and Yugoslavs which had been the basis of French policy
in the south-east. And Munich destroyed the Franco-Soviet pact.

On the other hand, the formation of the Axis created for France a
new potential threat in the south. German-Italian intervention in the
Spanish Civil War was aimed at adding yet another threat to those
already existing. The end of the Franco-Belgian alliance had exposed
her northern border. And German and Italian colonial claims imply

a grave threat to her colonial resources both of man power and of raw materials.

The recent *rapprochement* between Germany and France does not stand in contrast with these manifold threats, but is their logical sequel. The dangers France would run in case of an attack from the Axis have inclined her to come to terms with Germany, especially as at present the threat from Italy is more in the foreground. More exactly, these threats make one part of French public opinion amenable to German views and offers—the part, namely, represented by M. Bonnet, the Foreign Minister, and by M. Flandin, who, after having been a liberal, has today become an almost open advocate of the Fascist conception. In other words, the episode of Franco-German *rapprochement* is in itself a means of disintegrating French resistance. It must be added that these tendencies, which seemed extremely threatening in the months immediately after Munich, have since lost much of their strength, with the progress of British rearmament, with the stronger anti-German attitude in the United States, and with the German march into Prague.

The question important in our context is this: What are Germany's ultimate aims concerning France? Does she want to wreck France to the point of making her a German vassal State? The answer to this question is perhaps more simple than it seems. There is not the slightest reason to believe that the anti-French aims proclaimed in *Mein Kampf* have been discarded. Germany can never have a free hand in Eastern Europe, in Russia, or in Africa so long as France remains a great power. The French threat to German interests is not so dangerous today as it was ten or fifteen years ago, because France has become weaker since then. Yet France remains the chief obstacle to German colonial aims, and Germany will never put up with the threat of an attack in the west while she is pursuing her aims in the east.

But France can be driven from her position as a great power by means of what, in relation to Germany's insatiable thirst for expansion, appears almost as a limited programme. Undoubtedly Germany has designs upon a large slice of the French colonial possessions. Undoubtedly, too, Germany cannot feel herself secure in the west until the boundaries of France lie open to a military attack as do today the frontiers of Czecho-Slovakia. The fall of the French Maginot line is the logical counterpart to the fall of the Maginot line of Czecho-Slovakia. The iron-ore of Briey-Longwy (in Lorraine), which lies not far from the German border, was one of the most important German objectives even during the last war and has since become no less valuable. But all this does not imply a real dismemberment of France.

We leave the discussion of the colonial problem until a later chapter and here limit ourselves to the Maginot line. It is at this point that the anti-French movement in Alsace comes in. Undeniably Germany has guaranteed (or very nearly) the German-French border in the peace declaration drawn up between M. Bonnet and Herr von Ribbentrop in December 1938. But just during that period the French made very disagreeable discoveries in Alsace.

Before 1918, the Alsatians, though undoubtedly German in language, hated German rule. After 1918, they did not find themselves very happy under French rule either. The reasons for Alsatian uneasiness under France are not very easy to discover. Economically, the liberated territories had not much to complain about. And as to administration they had hated nothing so much as the truculent and contemptuous attitude of the officials from the German North. But once the change had come into effect, they began complaining about the irregularities which tend to go with French administrative methods. That this administration was largely in the hands of French civil servants, who could not even understand the local dialect, was a serious grievance. But the most serious aspect of the Alsatian problem was religious.

The greater part of Alsace is fervently Catholic, and the Catholic Church in Alsace enjoyed special rights incompatible with the separation of State and Church, which is such an essential element in

French democracy. Whereas in France religious teaching is rigorously excluded from all State-maintained educational institutions, all the schools in Alsace are run on a denominational basis. Twice since 1918 Left Wing Governments in France have made half-hearted attempts to bring Alsace into line with French religious legislation, but each time the attempt had to be given up in the face of fierce resistance on the part of the Alsatians. The attempts themselves had never been very serious, and once warded off need not constitute a lasting element of disturbance. Yet the fact remains that the Alsatians, at least the majority, distrust "atheist" France as much as Protestant Prussia. They feel really neither French nor German. They want to be as independent as possible.

Fairly soon after the War, a strong autonomous movement, representing all shades from mild home-rulers to unavowed separatists, grew up in Alsace. The autonomous movement proper was strongly Catholic, but the situation was made more complex through the emergence of a considerable Communist movement (dissident from Moscow) which took care not to offend too greatly the Catholics while flirting with Alsatian separatism. Strasbourg at one time had a Communist Mayor, who at the same time was an Alsatian separatist.

About 1930, things had somewhat quieted down, but the situation was again exacerbated in recent years. The depression, and the advent of the Nazis with the growing strength of Germany subsequent upon it, roused feelings to fever pitch. The depression in Alsace provided fuel for anti-Semitism. Alsace is the only region in France where the Jews matter, and unhappily they are for the most part money-lenders to the peasants. Anti-Semitism provided an easy means of access for the Nazis.

For a long time the Nazis carefully refrained from launching an organization of their own in Alsace. But since 1937 there has emerged the Elsass-Lothringische Partei, an exact counterpart to the Henlein party in Czecho-Slovakia. This party, just as the Henlein party, has a full-blown Nazi programme, with the one exception that so far it claims only full autonomy for Alsace and not its return to Germany.

No claim for separation could be raised without resultant trials for high treason.

What is much more important and much more unpleasant from the French point of view is the discovery made by the French authorities that there was grave suspicion that at least one outstanding leader of the Catholic autonomist movement was sympathetic with the German plot. He has recently been arrested on a charge of high treason, allegedly committed in the form of espionage on the behalf of Germany. The case in itself is not isolated. Vast German espionage organizations have been discovered in many countries, and German espionage normally goes hand in hand with attempts to create disturbances in the countries concerned and to foster Nazi movements on the German pattern. But the case is remarkable in so far as the accused man is neither a German nor an insignificant person but perhaps the most outstanding man in the autonomist movement in Alsace. It is not material for the political conclusions to be drawn from his arrest whether the charges brought against him are technically valid under French law. There can be little doubt about his political views, which were no secret and, just because they were not, involved not only himself personally but his party as well. It must be recognized that Nazi activities in Alsace have been much more successful than in Switzerland, and that Alsace is threatening to become a French Sudetenland.

Thus, amidst the Franco-German *rapprochement,* Germany is about to penetrate to the back of the Maginot line by political means. The outlines of the German aims in France become apparent. The goal is to destroy the power of France by annexing her border regions. Once this were done, Germany need not bother much about the rest. A Government of the extreme right, and very friendly to Germany, would be bound to come to the top, just as in Czecho-Slovakia, and Germany might then easily leave France to her own fate.

This undoubtedly is the German conception. Whether it will materialize is quite a different question. France wants to maintain her position as a great power and can hope to do so, so long as the co-operation of the three great democracies holds firm. She would certainly not be prepared to give up any part of her European territory. Before Germany could think of carrying out her plans, she would have to isolate France, put her under tremendous pressure, and break her resistance from within with the help of pro-German elements inside France. Such a situation may never come about. Yet if Germany wants to become the ruling power on the Continent, she can never cease aiming at just such a solution.

In this context, one more German minority must be mentioned; the Germans in South Tirol. Where the German element in Switzerland and the Flemish are intended to help in the encirclement of France, while Alsatian separatism is intended to break the backbone of her resistance, the Germans in South Tirol may be used as one among several means of keeping Italy loyal to the Axis policy.

The German minority in South Tirol is probably the worst-treated German minority in the world, with the possible exception of the Germans in Poland. The Italian policy of denationalization has been ruthless: the German language has been completely driven out of the schools (with the exception of religious instruction given in the native language as a concession to the Vatican), the leaders of German resistance against Italianization have long ago been punished by the usual Fascist means of cudgels and castor-oil, and the frontier has been lined with one long fence of barbed wire in order to cut off all contacts between South Tirol and the Germans across the border. Here, if anywhere, is a genuine grievance.

Numerically, the Germans in South Tirol are not important. They number only about a quarter of a million. Economically the little area is insignificant. Strategically it is very important because its southern border comes so close to the Italian Plain. The present border, running along the highest crest of the Alps, makes Italy reasonably safe from German attack. With German rule in Bozen (the chief town of the region) she would no longer be safe.

The feelings of the population are not so much nationalist as regionalist. They feel themselves not so much German as Tirolese.

But now that North Tirol belongs to Germany, regionalism has become identified for all practical purposes with German nationalism, and at the same time the *Anschluss* of Austria has sent a wave of hope through the oppressed region as through North Tirol itself.

All the democratic parties in Germany and every Austrian Government before the advent of the pro-Italian dictatorship of Dollfuss in 1934 have more or less supported the claims of the Germans in South Tirol. The Nazis, on the other hand, from their very beginning as a mass party in 1921, acted on a sort of diplomatic agreement with Mussolini (who at that time was not yet in power himself) never to touch on the South Tirol problem. Hitler has carefully kept to this policy, even after the *Anschluss*. But it is obvious that this policy holds good only so long as the Axis holds firm, and the possibility of raising the question of South Tirol at any time is one of the means of keeping Italy to the Axis policy. It is almost as if Hitler told Mussolini: If you don't ask for Nice from France, I shall ask Bozen (and other things) from you.

CHAPTER VII

THE SOUTH-EAST:
GERMAN METHODS OF EXPANSION

WE have finished our tour of the whole German border, listing all Germany's immediate claims. It may have seemed a strange approach to a study of the new German Empire. Germany's main interests at present seem to lie in the south-east, and it may therefore appear logical to begin with a description of German policy in the south-east and follow with a survey of Germany's more distant aims in the north, west, and south. But there is no saying in what direction Germany will turn next. One of the results of our survey, and one essential point about the new German Empire, is this, that its advance is equally important and threatening in every direction. Today it is Prague. Tomorrow it may just as well be Copenhagen, Amsterdam, Brussels, or Bern. Germany is not out for the domination of a limited zone of influence. She is striving after unlimited expansion.

Besides, in this study we are more concerned with the political methods of Germany than with any details of her most immediate aims. The aims and actions are in constant change, and what is said about them today will be out of date tomorrow. The methods of German expansion, however, are persistent, and as far as they undergo any material change, it is of great importance to understand the implications. Our survey has brought to light many aspects of these German methods of expansion which a study of conditions in the Balkans could not bring out very clearly. There are special conditions in the Balkans. The variety of conditions Germany meets in her expansion in all directions is alone able to bring out the features which are common to German methods in the midst of largely differing conditions.

The first thing which our survey has so far brought to light is that Germany takes her own borders as the starting point of her expansion. This is a fact of great importance. It applies equally to Japanese ex-

81

pansion and to the conquests made by Tsarist Russia. But it clearly distinguishes the German method of empire-building from that of Spain, Portugal, the Netherlands, Britain, France, the United States, and Italy. These latter empires conquered the weakest adversaries and the most valuable countries. Germany aims first of all at conquering her nearest neighbours.

We said that this aspect of German policy was similar to the policy of Japan and Tsarist Russia. But the similarity is superficial. Japan, in conquering Korea, Manchuria, Formosa, etc., really subjugated very weak countries, and the same applies to the Russian conquest of the Caucasus and of Turkestan. German expansion is directed against white nations, many of which must themselves be counted among the imperialist powers. The German problem is therefore different from any problem previously faced by the great powers of the west. It was one thing for Britain to conquer India. It is a task different in kind for Germany to conquer the Netherlands and Belgium. All methods must be entirely different in the two cases.

We shall see in later chapters that Germany's aims are by no means limited to Europe. On the contrary, German political theory today insists upon the dangers of a narrowly continental outlook and spurs Germany on towards becoming a "world power," creating an empire on the ruins of the supposedly decadent empires of Britain and France. That Germany and Japan are the natural heirs to Britain and France is the gist of every line written by Germany's most subtle and most influential political theorist, General Karl Haushofer.

But these wider aims (described as "oceanic" by Haushofer) Germany can tackle only after having solved her continental problems. This is a result of her geographical position. Germany cannot fight for colonies as Britain and France did. Britain could win supremacy in India and America with very little fighting on the Continent because she was mistress of the seas and had direct access to the overseas countries she wanted to conquer. England, owing to her unique geographic position, could afford to be one of the weakest powers on land, while at the same time the greatest world power. Germany, being an essentially continental country, cannot hope to rule the seas before ruling the Continent. She tried the opposite course before 1914, with disastrous results to herself.

Germany, therefore, cannot attempt to rule in the Near East, in Africa, and in South America so long as her domination of the Continent is threatened. But ruling the Continent is a task never before seriously faced by any great power. Louis XIV and Napoleon tried and failed. Will Hitler succeed any better?

Our survey has provided material showing how Germany is going about this task. The most outstanding feature is the subordination of her territorial conquests to the wider aims of indirect control. Territorial conquest was, on the whole, the final aim of Spain, France, Britain, etc. These older empires certainly knew that the possession of certain key positions guaranteed indirect control of wider areas. The English knew why they conquered the barren sites of Gibraltar and Aden, just as much as the Germans know why they put up a fight for such key positions as Memel and Bohumin. But finally, the key positions of the British served and serve the safe maintenance of British domination over the wide territories of India. It would be difficult to find a similar goal of territorial conquest for present German policy, though of course some such goal may emerge later. At present, however, territorial conquest for Germany is not so much an end in itself as a means of acquiring indirect control over wide areas. The acquisition of Memel and North Slesvig is intended to give her control over the Baltic and Scandinavia, the conquest of Alsace to give her control over all Western Europe, etc.

This predominance of the idea of indirect control in the German mind is obviously due to the fact that her victims so far are white people equal or superior to the Germans in civilization, on a level with herself in technique, and with a highly developed national consciousness.

Even to a Nazi mind, the idea of Germany's directly subjugating and suppressing all Europe, with a population many times her own, must seem fantastic. Indirect rule is therefore the only reasonable conception from the German point of view. Again, the term "indirect rule" must be used with caution, in order to avoid mistaken associations. It is one thing to control Hyderabad through its Sultan, and quite a different matter to control Belgium through the Flemish nationalist movement. The feature common to both is that domination is exerted through a power which has arisen within the dominated area itself and is in keeping with its local traditions.

It is quite a different question, however, whether indirect rule can be handled as easily in, say, Lithuania as it is in the Indian States. Or rather, even in the Indian States, indirect rule presents an increasingly difficult problem with the growth of Indian nationalism. It is an ideal system where the rule of the local potentate is unquestioningly accepted by his subjects, and a paramount power need do little more than secure his loyalty to herself. It is quite a different matter where local rule is in the hands of violent demagogic mass movements of the Nazi type which may easily change their mind, shift their allegiance, and escape control. In such cases, nothing remains to the paramount power but to step in by main force and establish her direct rule, which was just the thing to be avoided. Here, in a nutshell, is the problem of the German Empire. Can a system of indirect rule, however shrewdly and ruthlessly managed, hold good under the conditions of the European continent? And if not, what will be the fate of a Germany trying to oppress directly hundreds of millions of non-German Europeans? The conquest of Prague has pointed the question. The answer belongs to the future.

The problem for Germany is made more difficult by the very character of the Nazi regime itself. This regime explicitly denies equality to all non-Germans, subjecting them to the most ruthless oppression. Nazi Germany could never grant the Czechs equality for their language and national traditions. But she could not attempt to assimilate them either, because Germany rejects every policy of race mixture and attempts to keep her stock as racially pure as possible. It is true that the Czechs, though not Nordics, are at least "Aryans." Being neither Jews nor Negroes, their blood will not pollute the easily defiled purity of the Nazis. But in reality the nice points of racial theory do not matter. In practical politics the term "German" and "Nordic" merge, and to every good Nazi the Slavs are an inferior "race," though in the light of physical anthropology they are not a race at all but a linguistic group. Less than any other regime could a Nazi regime attempt to assimilate aliens, for by so doing she would bastardize the pure, proud Nordic stock.

Equality and assimilation being both out of the question, direct oppression remains the only alternative. It is an old trick of ruling groups to select a goodly number of talented people among their subjects and admit them to the ruling circle, thus nipping in the bud the movements of their adversaries. The Nazis could attempt such a policy less than any other regime. The result of their racialism is bound to be that they should keep their victims united in deadly hatred against themselves.

There is only one place, so far as I can see, where a white country has been systematically oppressed and assimilation systematically refused at the same time: Ireland. The results are known, but then Ireland had never more than eight million inhabitants, and did not occupy a strategically dangerous spot. Then too, despite all discriminatory legislation, the English system was never totalitarian, and for a hundred years the Irish Catholics sent their representatives to Westminster. Every alien nation directly conquered by Germany is bound to be several Irelands at once, with nothing but a Gestapo to offset the consequences.

But if direct rule over white people is made much more difficult by the Nazi system, indirect rule is made easier. Under the older political systems, an indirect rule over white people would have been inconceivable. It would have been impossible, in the long run, to rule a subject nation through a parliamentary regime, because democratic nationalism in the subject race would have immediately turned against the dominant power. But the case of the Nazi regime is different. Its peculiarities are such that it can hope to rule white people through indirect methods.

In Germany itself, the Nazis do not exclude the masses from politics. They force them into politics, canalizing their feelings by propaganda and cutting out unwanted influences through terrorism. The German regime could not subsist without either terrorism or propaganda. The Nazis may attempt to help similar regimes into the saddle in their vassal States.

It is a mistake to believe that propaganda can achieve everything. Its excessive use carries heavy penalties. No propaganda can succeed unless it appeals to certain fundamental impulses of its public. No propaganda can succeed when it runs counter to basic instinctive impulses. No German propaganda, for instance, will ever succeed with the Czechs, because it has no substantial arguments by which to appeal to them and because every Czech child carries in its blood the belief that the Germans are the natural enemies of the Czechs. Even where the chances of propaganda are better, success in the long run depends upon cutting out all criticism by means of terrorism.

Terrorism will certainly not be lacking in the countries Germany rules directly, but the appeal of propaganda in those countries will be nil. The case is entirely different, however, for local governments emerging from popular movements on the spot, adopting Nazi methods and dependent upon German support. Those governments can appeal to their nationals. Their rule may be just as much loved or hated— as the case may be—as the Nazi regime in Germany itself. In other words, Germany may hope to establish a system of indirect rule over large areas by spreading the Nazi revolution abroad.

Here world conquest and world revolution merge. For all the other approaches to power used by Germany—whether political, military, or economic—are subordinate to this one chief aim: to bring governments of the Nazi type to the top in other countries. It is an aim which cannot be fully achieved everywhere. But the possibility of bringing to the top a regime more or less similar to their own is nowhere excluded. Therefore Nazi expansion, almost by definition, cannot be limited to any definite area. Its scope is as wide as is the geographical extent of revolutionary potentialities. And there is no country in the world today whose political regime can be regarded as entirely safe. The crisis of democracy in Europe, the military dictatorships of South America, the collapse of old hierarchies in the East, all equally favour Nazi expansion.

The Nazi revolution today is the true world revolution. The days are past when the seat of world revolution was Moscow. The Communist International today is nothing but a bugbear, one more excuse for Nazi expansion. The Nazis have adopted the Communist concept of conquering the world through revolution. But they have made this concept more subtle, they have adapted it to nationalism, this dominating religion of our times, and thus made it acceptable where Communism had only been felt as an offence.

At this point the most immediate practical needs of the Nazi regime merge with its most profound impulses and its most distant aims into one single coherent whole. Nazi revolutions abroad are an immediate need of the regime, because Germany, to become a world power, must be master of the Continent and can rule it only through the spread of the Nazi revolution. But at the same time world revolution is the basic content of the Nazis' crusading faith. And Nazi world revolution in its turn must lead to Nazi world power, to the materializing of the distant dream of every German nationalist.

But it must again be emphasized: all this is dependent on Germany's ability to keep to the methods of indirect rule. As long as Germany is able to kindle the revolutionary fire, it will keep her soup warm. But direct German conquest is as sure to quench the revolutionary flame among her neighbours as her indirect influence is sure to fan it. Ruling Prague through Czech Fascists would have been one thing; ruling Prague through German violence is something quite different. Ruling Prague in the latter way will be costly enough; ruling the world by similar methods would be impossible.

Perhaps an analogy will help. The last successful attempt at uniting the whole known world in one empire was ancient Rome. And Rome saw to it that no civilized community should ever be ruled except by indirect methods, however harsh Roman rule may in fact have been.

The very few cases when the Romans departed from this method cost them a tremendous amount of blood and money. And when, after centuries of domination, Rome gradually abandoned the system of indirect rule for administrative centralization, she established apace equality between the Romans and their subject races. The belief in brute force alone which is always so near to the German political mentality is nothing but an evil superstition; as dangerous as the opposing anarchist superstition that man can be ruled by good-will alone.

Whether or not Germany can keep to her conception of indirect rule does not entirely or even primarily depend on the wishes of her leaders. It depends essentially on two points: can she give her subject races enough to keep their allegiance, can she balance the elements of consent and compulsion so as to produce the desired effect of keeping the willing allegiance of her vassals while keeping them in safe subjection?

It is a task which needs an enormous amount of strength but even more tact and judgment, two things which are not very conspicuous in the German political tradition. Empire-building is not a task for people with a deep-seated inferiority complex overcompensated by ferocity. The Germans during the last centuries have alternately been trampled upon or have trampled upon others. If they can be reproached with one thing it is their lack of balance. It is a natural result of their history. But even apart from psychological abilities and disabilities, the task is difficult enough.

Germany expands not for the sake of expansion only, however important expansion for its own sake may be in the Nazi conception of the world. She urgently needs economic advantages, in order to overcome the great economic difficulties to which her rearmament has exposed her. She wants to grasp gold and foreign exchange in kind. She needs foodstuffs and raw materials, and is unable to pay adequately for them. Here is the point where the famous German economic permeation of her neighbours comes in. It has found ample treatment in recent literature and has generally been regarded as the chief means of German expansion. This is a very doubtful contention.

It is obviously true that Germany by taking more than sixty per cent of Bulgaria's exports makes Bulgaria dependent upon her. If Germany at the same time contrives by artful devices to spoil the market for Bulgarian goods in other countries, Bulgaria's dependence upon Germany becomes more complete—in peace time. But the scheme loses its value in times of war. There would be no lack of markets for food and raw materials in war, and whether the economic ties prove an asset for Germany will then largely depend on whether German trade is a good bargain for her partners.

A look into any of the current text-books of German economic policy will convince every reader that they consist of a description of German methods in sharp dealing. And methods of sharp dealing so far have never proved good for making friends. It is true that economic expansion is bound to be one of the most important aims of German imperialism, but whether it is a means of cementing her incipient empire is quite a different question.

In practice the answer to this question cannot be a simple yes or no. The effect of German trade policy upon various classes of the population is very different. And Germany's special trade methods tend to develop these differences among her customers to sharp antagonism which, in its turn, is a political advantage for her.

Wherever she can, Germany buys whole crops or the entire output of a certain raw material in a certain country in bulk. She claims to pay higher prices for these purchases than could be obtained on the world market. It is in the matter of these prices that the discriminatory effect of German trade policy has its roots. The prices Germany pays are fixed in the local currency, and in this local currency they are high. It is in local currency that the producers receive pay. The growers of Hungarian and Rumanian and Yugoslav wheat, of Bulgarian and Greek tobacco, of Greek and Turkish cotton, of Turkish raisins, of Rumanian oil seeds, etc., can only be pleased at getting higher prices from Germany than they would get from any other customers. And the producers of Rumanian oil, Yugoslav iron-ore, copper, lead, zinc, etc., together with their workers, can only share these feelings.

Unfortunately, the prices are paid at the expense, not of Germany but of other sections of the population of the countries concerned. First of all, Germany fixes an exchange rate, varying from country to country, and sometimes even from transaction to transaction, but always extremely favourable to herself. The goods are paid for not in money but in German goods. And owing to the exchange rate, which overvalues the mark, these goods in their turn are delivered at high prices. This, at least, is so where Germany has no competitors to fear. In the other case she is able to follow a policy of ruthless undercutting both directly by unlimited State subsidies for exports and by clever adaptation of her exchange rates to the necessities of the situation.

The exporters to Germany do not get their money from Germany at all. For one of the interminable complaints about Germany is that, as soon as she is in a strong position, her deliveries fall far into arrears as against her purchases. In the meantime the Balkan peasants are paid in high sums by their respective State banks. And the man who in reality pays for the margin between German prices and world market prices is certainly not the German importer but the man who buys German goods and the national banks of the countries concerned; in other words, the taxpayer. This, of course, is only the general position. As long as there are serious competitors in the field, the situation is very different, and the bargains are really favourable to those dealing with Germany.

In these circumstances it is obvious that the importers and the financiers of the countries concerned are the groups severely hit by German trade policy. The situation of the importers is often disastrous. Here again the picture varies. Germany, after all, must offer something for her purchases, and she makes her best offers precisely to those groups which provide her with products important to herself. Germany has always been prepared to deliver machinery for the improvement of the output of raw material and agriculture in the countries concerned. Big German offers for the development of Yugoslav mining, Greek and Turkish cotton-growing, and Rumanian oil production are within recent memory. Here Germany is developing her own resources. But the picture is different where this is not the case.

First of all, Germany increasingly attempts to offer what she describes as "credits." It is a nice sort of credit indeed. A country devoid of money, as Germany is, cannot give credits. Her so-called "credits" consist in undertakings to deliver installations for the construction of new plant, within long terms up to ten years' time, while at the same time regularly receiving the crops and mineral outputs of the countries concerned. It is easy to see that these "credits" are not given by Germany to her partners but the other way round. Germany promises future completion of certain works against immediate deliveries from her partners. And the latter are then tied for many years and cannot change their commercial policy, because otherwise the German constructions would remain unfinished.

But this is not the worst aspect of German trade policy. Her partners need goods for consumption. And Germany is unable to deliver these goods, especially textiles. Thus the countries concerned must put up with receiving in exchange for their valuable deliveries, goods such as aspirin, harmonicas, radio sets, etc., for which they do not provide a real market. They must accept goods of extremely low and constantly declining quality, many of them, such as engines and armaments, actually scrapped in Germany. And finally they must accept increasing delays in delivery.

The governments, the banks, and the importers in these countries therefore have a natural tendency to break away from the German market. And Germany must evolve complex and clever, if somewhat objectionable, devices for keeping them to the German market. The simple method originally applied rested on the golden rule that there is no stronger position in the world than that of a man who threatens his creditors with complete default. Germany imported heavily from her neighbours without paying either in money or in kind, thus running up a heavy balance against herself. Then she suddenly made the covering of this balance dependent upon further deliveries of foodstuffs and raw materials and upon the purchase of useless or inferior German goods. It was a method applied against almost every one of her neighbours, and followed to the point where her partners, in despair and disregarding all possible consequences, refused to deliver further goods to Germany until the balance was covered. Yugoslavia was the worst case, and it is there that political resentment against Germany on account of her somewhat unusual trade methods has been strongest.

On the whole, Germany now tends to abandon these methods in favour of others. One new method is the one already mentioned, that of giving "credits." Another springs from the German method of buying certain products in bulk and supplying her partners with certain goods to the exclusion of all competitors. Germany then has a free hand to re-export what surplus remains in her hands and makes ample use of it. Having paid on an exchange rate extremely favourable to herself, she can dump these surpluses on the world market and still make a profit. Her partners may in turn arrange to dispose of the surplus goods they received. They may dump them on the world market, too, and there is a beautiful story of how Greek tobacco sold by Germany suddenly appeared on the world market at ridiculous prices while German guns, sold by the Greek Government at the same time, appeared in Barcelona to defend the Spanish Republican Government.

But one thing is certain: Germany's partners may dump German surplus goods of inferior quality on the international markets while they can no longer sell there their own staple products because German dumping of their own goods has irremediably spoiled the market for them. Now an iron chain binds them to Germany.

There is one more tie of a similar kind. Once Germany has by artful devices laid her hands on the greater part of a country's exports, this country is linked to barter methods, owing to the lack of free exchange, which is the result of bartering her staple products to Germany. All countries trading on a large scale with Germany are now starved of free exchange. And the scarcity of free exchange in turn makes them more dependent upon German imports which are granted through barter, however objectionable these German imports may be in kind and quality.

There could be only one remedy for this situation. It would change from one day to the next if countries disposing of free exchange would buy a substantial proportion of the exports of the countries concerned. But for this there does not seem to be much hope at present. The basic situation thus created can be expressed in exceedingly simple terms. Germany is constantly growing in importance as an importer. But she cannot really pay for what she imports. And with her rearmament continuing at an ever more fantastic speed, she becomes increasingly unable to pay decently for what she consumes. That is why all Germany's trade devices directly or indirectly lead to a ruthless exploitation of her partners.

No country would agree to such a transaction could it find adequate markets elsewhere. But even as things are, Germany must use special devices for keeping her partners to their side of the agreement. Some of these devices, as described above, are of an economic character. But the basic device, that of buying certain products in bulk and enforcing high payment to the producers in local currency, at the expense of other groups and of the taxpayer, is essentially a political device. It links the landed and mining interests of the countries concerned to Germany. And if finance and trade may often have the ear of the Government, it is the peasants who give the big battalions to every mass movement in the Balkans.

Thus, after an excursion into economics, we are back again at politics. Economic penetration in itself is a double-edged sword. In the long run it is as likely to impoverish as to develop the countries concerned. It may artificially develop certain of their resources, but is bound to curtail heavily their state of supplies. In itself German economic expansion is as much a political danger to Germany as English vested interests in Ireland or India were apt to rouse the hostility of the natives.

But the German reaction to this danger is on the whole exactly the contrary of what the English reaction was before the introduction of self-government and even after. The older empires invariably tried to take the small ruling stratum into their interest. It was an excellent policy in the beginning, and still is in backward areas. But where modern mass movements arise, its value decreases. Germany, true to the Nazi tradition, aims at tying to her interest the peasant as against the upper classes.

Yet this alone would certainly not be sufficient to keep her neighbours under her control. She must bring direct pressure to bear upon the governments concerned and the business groups which closely co-operate with these governments. For this aim Germany has many levers. Paramount among them is the direct military threat which Germany can now exert against every small country in Europe, but especially in the east and south-east. This point needs no further elaboration. More than once, as in the case of the barter agreement for Hungarian wheat and for Rumanian oil, such military threats have been brought directly to bear upon Germany's trade partners.

Another means, more gentle but no less efficient, is German supplies of armaments. In view of the need for uniform training, no army can easily work with armaments of different origin. Once Germany has offered or forced upon some country vast supplies of arms, she can be pretty sure that the country concerned will have to follow her international policy. Since the conquest of the Skoda works in Czecho-Slovakia, there is no south-eastern country to which this situation does not apply, though Rumania and Yugoslavia tried to extricate themselves from the clutches of Germany.

This leads up to the use of these armaments. The countries concerned mostly need arms against one another. The entire east and south-east of Europe is filled with terrific hatreds, beginning with the blood-feud between Poles and Lithuanians and ending with the Bulgarian claims upon Greek territory. Hungary's and Bulgaria's claims for revision spread an element of unrest over the whole area. In the present state of things, no frontier in these parts of the world is likely to remain untouched, but none can be revised without German toleration at least. Thus every government must try to remain in Germany's good graces, and the Nazis can apply the golden maxim of "divide and rule."

In this contest German policy, in accordance with the Nazi faith, has been to make linguistic boundaries coincide with the borders of the various countries. But the uneven boundaries of the linguistic units bear no relation to the economic and strategic needs of the various Balkan countries, and are therefore most irrational. Even the winning side in the fight for boundary revision is apt to be more helpless and dependent on foreign help afterwards than before. Besides, no borderline can be drawn so that no minorities remain on either side. The antagonisms between these small countries are therefore doomed to be perpetual, and to throw their governments into the arms of Germany.

It must be finally noted, and this is a very important point, that at home all the governments concerned are very weak. In almost every one of the eastern and south-eastern countries the existing military and police dictatorships are threatened either by a Fascist movement on the Right or by a revolutionary peasant movement on the Left, or by both simultaneously. Sometimes, as in the case of Hungary, the Fascist movement itself is to a large extent a revolutionary peasant movement. All this provides splendid opportunities for Germany. While the creation of Nazi regimes in these countries remains her ultimate goal, she is not loath in the meantime to reap what advantage she can from the pressure wrought by various mass movements upon military and bureaucratic governments which cannot hope to subsist without German support.

In this context, the fight of various linguistic groups within one country has special significance. Sometimes linguistic groups have a country of their own across the border and then their claims coincide with the case for border revision. But in several cases these groups have no country of their own abroad, and the effect of their mutual strife is all the more disruptive. This was the case of the Slovaks in Czecho-Slovakia and is still the case of the Croats in Yugoslavia and, in a slightly different sense, of the Ukrainians in Poland. Here we touch again the problem of the mass movements, for movements such as those of the Croats and Ukrainians are not the affair of the Government but of masses hating it. It is one of those cases where the Germans, by means of threats and inducements, try to win over governments while at the same time launching mass movements against them. The Slovak and Ukrainian mass movements were backed by Germany for a long time. Now Germany has begun backing the Croats.

But this is certainly not the only case where Germany stirs up intense nationalism. One of two chief means used for launching Nazi movements is precisely the spreading of the hectic sort of nationalism which dominates her own country. The other is the stirring up of social revolution to varying degrees.

As to social revolution, it is easy to stir it up where no agrarian reform has been introduced. But in most parts of Eastern and South-Eastern Europe ample agrarian reforms have been carried out since 1918. The fight of the underdog against the rich is, however, invariably present in all agitation stimulated by the Nazis, and finds a strong expression in her commercial policy as described above. It is sheer nonsense to think of the Nazis as fundamentally opposed to social revolution. Here again there exists a fundamental difference between the Nazi empire and all former empires. All the old empires, believing in a hierarchy, allied themselves to the upper classes in their colonies. Germany seeks support indiscriminately where she can get it.

As to nationalism, the difference between Germany and the older empires is again remarkable. All older empires were invariably hostile to the emergence of nationalism among their subject races. They are therefore threatened by its rise in their colonies. The Nazis stir up nationalism to fever heat, invariably backing the most extreme and unreasonable version of it. It is nationalism of this sort which guarantees that the revolutionary movements they try to launch will remain under their control and not fall under the control of the Comintern. Conversely, the strength of nationalist feeling prevents the

Comintern from having any real successes in Europe and drives revolutionary movements into the arms of the Fascists.

Nationalism and social revolution, in the east and south-east, merge and culminate in anti-Semitism. Anti-Semitism is an aspect of Nazism, the importance of which for the German penetration of the east of Europe can never be overrated. For the Jewish problem is much more real in these parts than in Germany. In Germany, the Jews never had the influence the Nazis pretended to believe they had. But east of Germany the position is different. Whereas the Jews in Germany numbered less than one per cent, there are very considerable Jewish minorities in Lithuania, Poland, the Ukraine, Slovakia, Hungary, Rumania, Vienna, and Istanbul. In Vienna the Jews numbered ten per cent of the population; in Budapest they number twenty per cent; in Lodz, the second principal city in Poland, they numbered until recently forty-eight per cent, and in the smaller country towns farther to the east the proportions sometimes rise to seventy or eighty per cent of the total. The nations of the east and south-east until recently consisted of a landed aristocracy and their peasantry. The towns were Jewish to an extraordinary degree. With the rise of the modern industrial system, one section of the Jews almost automatically acquired predominance in business and in the professions. And the rising middle class of the peoples of the east and south-east therefore meets the Jew as its most obvious competitor.

That the Poles, Hungarians, Rumanians, etc., should develop a middle class of their own is a natural and desirable process. Its effects upon eastern Jewry are inevitably unpleasant. The situation has been made much more difficult by the restrictions imposed upon immigration in the United States. And now the situation in Palestine is liable to close the last large-scale outlet. Thus, no less than seven million Jews are bottled up in an area where most of them are no longer wanted. It is a problem fraught with terrible implications. These Jewish masses had somehow managed to live under relatively prosperous conditions in the old Austrian and Russian Empires. In the cramped conditions of their successor States they are the most obvious objects of discrimination in any economic difficulty. Moreover, the excited nationalism of the young peoples of the south-east can never be fully satisfied, precisely because in actual fact they are all more or less vassals to Germany and cannot obtain full satisfaction for their high-flown aspirations. So the hatreds they cannot fully express in their actions against their neighbours quite naturally turn against the Jew as a helpless scapegoat.

With good-will on all sides, and international co-operation, the problem of eastern Jewry would not be insoluble. But these are factors almost completely absent from the present situation, and the Nazis are busy stirring up the worst instincts of human nature against the Jew. There is little doubt that within a few years the fate of the Jews in Eastern Europe will resemble that of the Armenians in Turkey.

Anti-Semitism is an excellent means for the Nazification of the nationalist movements east of Germany. The Jews being so large a section of the business and professional classes of the countries concerned, their extermination is in itself a measure of social revolution. The anti-Semitic movement in Slovakia or Hungary or any other of these countries is essentially a movement of peasants and their university-trained sons against the urban bourgeoisie. In the east, the racial and religious aspect of anti-Semitism thinly veils the battle cry of social upheaval. Besides—and this is perhaps the most important aspect of the whole problem—the Jewish section of the upper classes in the east is inextricably intertwined with the non-Jewish sections. The Hungarians, for instance, find it difficult to provide an anti-Semitic leader without a Jewish grandmother, and at least one of the most outstanding anti-Semitic leaders in Hungary is himself a half-Jew. The bonds between the Jewish bourgeoisie and the non-Jewish gentry are very close. Anti-Semitism in its extreme Nazi version, therefore, threatens the upper classes as a whole.

Nationalism, being practically identical with anti-Semitism in these parts of the world, is extremely liable to fall under the Nazi sway. But there are other aspects of nationalism. It is naturally opposed to the international ideologies of Marxism, communism, socialism. It is opposed to all sorts of pacifism, including the liberal and democratic belief in compromise. And in the European east and south-east, ideas to a very large extent have always been imported from Germany. It is a small step indeed from the native brands of anti-Semitic nationalism to full-fledged Nazism.

One important element in the picture is the German minorities. In no single country in Europe except France do they number more than several hundred thousand. But wherever Germany is able to do so, and especially in the east and south-east, they are organized as a State within the State on strict Nazi lines. Germany claims a sort of extra-territoriality for them so that they need not care for the laws of their respective countries in carrying out their political agitation. They are a spearhead of the Fascist movement and provide a constant possibility of raising quarrels about alleged disregard for their special rights.

We have now drawn the picture of the German conception of indirect rule as applied all over Europe, but with particular concentration in the east and south-east. It is a conception profoundly different from that of older empires. It may be defined as a conception of empire-building in an era of democratic mass movements. This concise formula certainly needs elaboration. The older empires, as we saw, were thoroughly authoritarian and anti-democratic. When they were formed, the mother countries themselves were just emerging from the rule of strong hierarchies into the beginnings of liberalism and democracy. They ruled their empires as they had themselves been ruled a hundred years before. It is this that now constitutes their weakest spot. Here lies the chief advantage of the Nazis. They can start with methods which others can achieve by a difficult process of adaptation.

But is it not a paradox to contrast the Nazi type of empire-building as "democratic" with that of the older empires as "authoritarian"? Is not the Nazi regime more authoritarian than any other? In a sense it is. But it would be as one-sided to describe it as purely authoritarian as to describe it as democratic. The Nazi regime is a ruthless and ferocious autocracy, built on an equally ferocious mass movement of the underdogs. The Nazi regime is certainly not a regime of democratic liberalism. It is a regime of "democratic" Cæsarism, of Cæsarism based on demagogy.

What does this mean in terms of empire-building? Britain has succeeded to an extent in building up a liberal democratic empire. Her success was complete in the case of those dominions which are Anglo-Saxon in race and language. But the farther away her subjects are from Anglo-Saxon race and tradition, the more difficult become the problems of imperial democracy. The democratic mass movements in India and in the Arabic countries have a tendency not to cement but to threaten the empire. At any rate, the introduction of liberal democracy into the colonies means the loosening of the ties of empire, and this all the more, the more distant a colony is in tradition and outlook from the motherland.

A totalitarian regime holds out greater hopes of making mass movements subservient to the keeping down of these very masses who support them. Should the Nazi Governments in Germany's various vassal countries be sufficiently strong, she need, as we said, only secure the allegiance of the Governments themselves. Mass movements will not threaten her in totalitarian countries dependent upon her support. Yet the question remains: Will this ideal type of German imperialism —a commonwealth of Fascist nations under German domination— ever materialize?

The scheme may miscarry where nations refuse to submit to Germany and become Fascist. For such a refusal there can be many reasons. The old rulers of a country may successfully resist the onslaught of Fascist revolution. The strength of a Fascist movement in a country may be broken, either because Germany tends to exploit the country too ruthlessly economically or because she refuses to give full satisfaction to her national aims, or because Germany, impatient with the intricacies of indirect rule, steps in too openly as the real master. If it is a country helplessly exposed to German aggression, resistance will force the Germans to abandon their concept of indirect rule and make them turn to direct conquest. If it is a country with a certain power of resistance and a chance of finding support among the other great powers, a potential ally will turn into a potential enemy. These possibilities are crucial. We shall study them a little more closely in the subsequent sections.

Germany's first experiment with indirect rule, the one in Czecho-Slovakia, has at any rate been thrown out of gear.

CHAPTER VIII

THE SOUTH-EAST: CZECHO-SLOVAKIA

It was the wrecking of Czecho-Slovakia at Munich which finally opened the doors of the south-east to Germany. German penetration of the Balkans had started long before Hitler, acquired greater momentum after the advent of the Nazis, but did not come to a head before 1938. Up to 1938 the Balkans were still primarily an Italian zone of influence, with Austria and Hungary as Italian bastions protecting the countries further removed from Germany against German aggression. The fall first of Austria and then of Czecho-Slovakia broke these barriers. The German strongholds in Vienna and Prague provide just that element of physical threat to all the Balkan countries without which no German control of this wide area would be conceivable.

But the tragedy of Czecho-Slovakia, besides its international implications, is well worth studying for its own sake. Czecho-Slovakia is the country which, of all the minor powers around Germany, first fell under complete German vassalage. In one sense, in Czecho-Slovakia, Germany scored the greatest success she has so far achieved. But in another, it is very doubtful whether Germany has reached, in Czecho-Slovakia, just the goal at which she was aiming. Czecho-Slovakia shows in full all the methods of German expansion with their strong and their weak points.

Throughout the period leading up to the Munich crisis there was an element of disproportion in the presentation of the Czech situation abroad. All the time it appeared as if it were a triangular contest among the Sudetenlanders, the Czechs, and the Germans, with the other great powers ready to interfere. Relatively little was said about the dissensions within the Czech camp, about the difficulties against which Beneš had to struggle. In fact Czech resistance was broken up at least as much from within as from without. The conservative section of Czech political opinion sympathized strongly with Henlein and Hitler. These groups had a strong representation in the Agrarian Party. The leader of this Right Wing was Beran, the chairman of the party itself. The Prime Minister, Hodža, inclined more towards Beneš. But it was Beran and not Hodža who was the real master of the Agrarians.

The Agrarian Party had originally been a secondary political force, representing the wealthy peasants. Gradually, thanks to a series of extremely able leaders, it managed to become the point of concentration of all the conservative forces: landowners, bankers, industrialists. The army always remained a stronghold of the Left, but the civil service became practically an instrument of the Agrarian Party.

The Czecho-Slovak Republic was founded in 1918 on the principles of a progressive, democratic nationalism. President Masaryk was almost a moderate Socialist. Beneš had always been his right-hand man. The army had believed in both. The working-class organizations were strong. The rise of the Agrarian Party to power had pushed these Leftist tendencies somewhat into the background, but its rule could not be secure so long as the presidential office and the army were in the hands of its adversaries.

The Left in Czecho-Slovakia comprised those groups which had been most strongly anti-Austrian and most strongly nationalist. The Agrarians had never been very anti-Austrian even before 1918 and were not very nationalist afterwards. Subsequent developments drew them nearer to the Sudetenlanders. The large landowners were mostly aristocrats who could be regarded neither as Czech nor as German. They were international. At the same time they were among the strongest supporters of the Agrarian Party. The great Czech banks were sometimes inextricably involved with the affairs of the German industrialists in the Sudetenland. Politically the Right Wing of the Agrarians felt themselves to be nearer to Henlein than to Beneš. Nationally they were readier to put up with German claims than was the Beneš group. Not very democratic themselves, they took a sober view of the international situation and did not believe in the willingness of the western democracies to help. The only reasonable policy, in their opinion, was to come to an understanding with Henlein. They would rule Czecho-Slovakia together with him on an autocratic system, as a dependency of Germany.

They were far from being Fascists. They were only very mildly anti-democratic, not unconscious of the honour of their Czech nation, scarcely in any way anti-Semitic. They thought that by giving in to Henlein they could keep things within limits. This belief they shared with Lord Runciman, with Mr. Chamberlain, and with M. Bonnet.

At the decisive hour, the Czechs had forty divisions, their Maginot line, and the expectation of Russian help in the air. If they could hold out for a few weeks—as they would probably be able to do—they had some hope of forcing Russia, France, and Britain to join in. It would have been a desperate gamble. But the opposite course was certain perdition. The Agrarians prevented the Left from taking this chance.

But their hopes were not fulfilled. Hitler had only dangled the hope of a Beran-Henlein coalition Government before their eyes. Instead of maintaining Czecho-Slovakia intact under Nazi-Agrarian rule, he annexed the Sudetenland. Beran found himself Prime Minister—of a hopelessly truncated country.

He accepted the task on a political calculation which at the outset did not seem to be entirely mistaken. Czecho-Slovakia was still a country of about ten million inhabitants with many economic and strategic assets. Of these ten millions, about seven millions were Czechs who would not willingly put up with German domination. There is no other people in Eastern Europe like the Czechs. They are of a stubbornness, a tenacity, of a firmness and continuity of purpose, of a rudeness of manner which are truly Prussian. At the same time their Slavonic feelings are stronger than those of any other Slav people. They hate the Germans by instinct and tradition, and their level of political and general education is higher than that of any other eastern nation; they cannot easily be browbeaten into submission.

Under such conditions Germany must wish to rule Czecho-

Slovakia through an autonomous Government which would have a substantial backing among the Czechs themselves. The Beran Government seemed to be what the Germans needed. And Beran could hope that in compensation for his pro-German attitude in international politics he would be able to prevent Germany from squeezing the last drop of blood out of Czecho-Slovakia. No more strongly pro-German Government with any mass backing was to be had in Czecho-Slovakia. Thus the Germans would be obliged to take into account the wishes of Beran.

The new regime had an astonishingly easy start. Munich was accompanied by a violent reversal of feelings in Czecho-Slovakia. The Czechs had always been sincere democrats but much more nationalist than democratic. When their nationalism came into conflict with their democratic views, they sacrificed the latter without much hesitation. National survival after Munich was dependent upon getting along somehow with Germany. They settled down to the task. The democracies had let them down. They turned to hating and despising the democracies. In the days which followed Munich, Englishmen and Frenchmen found it uncomfortable to speak their own languages in the streets of Prague. Strangely enough, there was no real feeling of resentment against Germany. The Germans had done what it was natural they should try to do. The Czechs would now try to get on with the Germans.

Within five months, Germany managed to waste this moral capital until she was reduced to the use of main force. It is not in the character of the Nazi regime (as little as of any previous German regime, except the Weimar Republic) to be generous to the defeated and gentle to the weak. The Nazi regime, in particular, cannot envisage the weak and defeated in any other role than that of an outlet for their sadistic instincts. It is here that the Nazi mentality differs most profoundly from that of all the great empire-builders.

Parcere subjectis et debellare superbos. (Curb the proud, but when you have subjected them treat them with humanity.) This was the principle on which the Roman Empire was built, on which every empire has to be built. Constant neglect of either part of this rule invites disaster. Empires crash if they are unwilling to fight their enemies. They crash, too, if they cannot transform a military conquest into peaceful administration. It is the second score on which Germany is likely to fail in the execution of her plans.

In the case of Czecho-Slovakia, the methods of bullying culminated in the cheap triumph of marching German troops into defenceless Prague, but these methods led to the miscarriage of clever and far-reaching plans of much greater importance, as we shall see in a moment. But it was not entirely due to the *furor teutonicus*. The Germans are themselves in such desperate straits economically that they simply had to squeeze Czecho-Slovakia to the last drop of blood; and in order to do this they had to get full control of the Czech resources. It is here that the final conflict originated.

All the other reasons given for the German march into Prague are partly excuses and only of secondary importance. The chief reason for the final German conquest was the insatiable hunger of Germany for gold and foreign exchange. The Austrian gold reserve had been spent. The trade deficit was increasing catastrophically. A reduction of rearmament was out of the question. Britain's offer to negotiate a trade agreement which would have given German exports a wider market was dependent upon Germany's keeping to what the British Government described as the "spirit of Munich." This the Nazis did not want. The only alternative was to lay their hands on a new gold-reserve by main force. Like the Spanish *conquistadores,* the Nazis conquer helpless enemies in an interminable hunt after gold. Their economic system can exist only by dint of constant levies upon their supposed enemies.

Gold indeed there is in Czecho-Slovakia. The spoils in Czecho-Slovakia will be greater than in poor Austria. The gold reserve of the Czech National Bank alone amounts to about thirty million pounds. There must be private reserves, too, and there is every reason to believe that the Germans will despoil the Czechs almost as thoroughly as they have despoiled the Jews.

No statistics are available for the region now occupied by Germany as distinct from the other parts of former Czecho-Slovakia. But this much is certain: Czech Bohemia and Moravia have an agricultural surplus, especially in wheat, which will help Germany considerably. Germany acquired a few mines, and very important steelworks which will help her rearmament. With the Skoda works she acquired the largest arms-exporting concern in Europe. And the Bata works in Zlin dominate the world shoe market. There is reason to believe that the conquest of the Czechs will help to reduce, to a certain extent, Germany's permanent trade deficit. And the acquisition of the gold-reserve will be sufficient to tide Germany over many difficulties for a year or even more. Germany can continue unhampered to build her bombers.

But it is another question whether Germany has not paid dearly for these advantages. A brief survey of the road that led Hitler to Prague will show the implications.

The original German conception was, as explained above, that Beran, with the support of all the conservative forces, should rule Czecho-Slovakia for them. And in order to avoid any tricks on his part, the Germans had the Slovaks and Ruthenians ready. One of the first consequences of Munich was the introduction of home rule for Slovakia and for Ruthenia, renamed the Carpatho-Ukraine.

The problems concerning these two little countries with two million and less than one million inhabitants, respectively, are too complex for detailed description. But this much must be said, that a mistaken impression is created by the current representation of the Slovaks' and the Ruthenians' opposing the Czechs as united peoples with a nationalism of their own. A decisive fact about both Slovakia and Ruthenia is that political consciousness there, in contrast to the Czechs, has not yet penetrated down to the masses. In Ruthenia to this day this statement applies in an almost absolute sense. The unhappy little country has seen no less than three waves of refugees drift in since 1914: Jews, Russians, and Ukrainians. And what political agitation there is, is mainly due to these refugees, among the utter indifference of the still largely illiterate and extremely wretched peasantry. The Ruthenian peasant feels no real allegiance to any social group except the community of his particular valley. He does not care whether he is under the rule of Czechs, Hungarians, Poles, Ukrainians, Russians, or Germans.

Political indifference is not so absolute among the Slovaks. But their most active section always was the Protestant minority, who happened to be mostly pro-Czech. The Catholic majority before the War put up with Hungarian rule without much resentment, however oppressive it was. In fact they minded the ruthless Hungarian landlord and the corrupt Hungarian administration less than the Czech civil servant who came in after the War and brought with him agrarian reform. For the Slovaks, the Czechs were too thorough and uncomfortable. The young generation after the War gradually grew into a Slovak nationalism strongly hostile to the Czechs. It is not a very broad movement, however. Its importance was derived not so much from its own strength as from the absence of any very active counterforce.

It was this absence of the real participation of the masses in politics which made it easy for the Germans to get control of Slovakia and Ruthenia after Munich. In the case of Ruthenia, they had only to choose whether to back the Ukrainian or the Russian refugees. They decided on the former in view of the pressure a Ukrainian national movement backed by Germany could exert upon Poland, and in view of a future disruption of the Soviet Union by the Ukrainian national movement. German advisers organized the young Ukrainians into the SIC, a sort of Ukrainian Storm Troops. There was no resistance within the country against their rule.

What resistance there was came from without and not on the part of the Czechs. The Czechs were only too happy to help the Germans and Ukrainians to keep the country in a very loose federation with Czecho-Slovakia. The threat to the Ukrainian movement came from Hungary and Poland, with the indirect support of Russia, Rumania, and Italy. Hungary and Poland wanted a common boundary, and

Italy backed the claim because it would lead to the reconstitution of a barrier of smaller powers against the German advance in the south-east. Poland and Russia had an obvious interest in crushing the SIC, which contemplated the disruption of both countries. For Hungary, the claim to Ruthenia was part of her general claim for treaty revision, for the return to Hungary of all territories lost after the War. This Hungarian claim extended to both Slovakia and Ruthenia, but was easier to achieve in the case of Ruthenia, owing to the indifference of the local population. German, Czech, and Ukrainian interests in Ruthenia confronted the interests of all the other powers from Italy to Soviet Russia.

The case of Slovakia was simpler. Here the Germans helped to strengthen an already existing defence organization of the Slovak autonomists, the Hlinka Guards. Immediately after Munich the Hlinka Guards took over power in Slovakia with practically no resistance from any side. They established a sort of totalitarian regime, abolishing all parties except their own and driving out the Jews and Czechs. But within the Slovak autonomous movement there were serious divergences of view. Slovakia, like Ruthenia, is much too poor to live on her own resources. There is no party of independence in Slovakia. Some elements inclined towards the maintenance of federal links with the Czechs, others towards a return to Hungary under some federal constitution, others wanted to make Slovakia a German protectorate.

The Germans very successfully confronted the Hungarian party and its Italian and Polish friends. In November 1938 the problem of Slovakia and Ruthenia came under joint German-Italian arbitration. The result was that Hungary recovered about one million inhabitants with most of the larger towns and the most important railways and roads of both provinces as well as the most fertile lowlands. But Slovakia and Ruthenia, deprived of their granary, of important road and railway communications, and of most of their towns, remained only more helplessly dependent upon Germany for all that. Germany has preserved her spearhead, the eastern part of Czecho-Slovakia, pointing towards Rumania, the Black Sea, and the Soviet Ukraine.

Thus Germany has acquired, within Czecho-Slovakia, two small vassal States which did not at all mind their vassalage. It is a characteristic case of south-eastern psychology. In its independence, Ruthenia remained in utter wretchedness. Slovakia, instead of the mild rule of the Czechs, had now accepted the harsh rule of the Germans. It gave them a chance of venting their resentment against their nearest kin and neighbour, the Czechs. As to the Czechs themselves, the three million Slovaks and Ruthenians under German orders would be sufficient to keep them to the German allegiance. And they must even be grateful to Germany for having kept these two provinces within the borders of a federal Czecho-Slovakia against the Hungarian claims. There seemed to exist a solid basis for German-Czech collaboration.

This collaboration was wrecked by excessive German demands. The Germans obtained a road through Czecho-Slovakia under German sovereignty which cut the republic in two. They obtained the right for the German minority to organize on Nazi lines. They obtained an unlimited prorogation of the Czech parliament. They obtained the cancelling of the Czech tariff for Sudetenland goods. But every new concession on the part of the Czechs only led to new German claims.

The Germans claimed special rights on the Czech railways. They claimed a leading part in the administration for the German minority, about one-hundredth of the population after Munich. They claimed a purging of the army from all independent-minded commanders. They claimed the introduction of the German type of anti-Semitism. They claimed part of the Czech gold-reserve as a cover for the Czech currency in the Sudetenland, while refusing to take over a proportionate part of the Czech debt. They aired the idea of a customs and currency union with Germany.

All these claims were a tremendous justification after the event for the Beneš policy. His old partisans were fairly strongly entrenched in the army and in the diplomatic service. They had their outposts in the administration, and with growing German demands the divergence between the Beneš and the Beran groups appeared increasingly insignificant. Germany had contrived to unite the Czech nation again against her.

The real danger for Germany arose out of the international contest in which this Czech resistance evolved. Ever since January 1939, from Spain to Rumania, the German policy had encountered reverses. If Germany was not even able to put down resistance in Prague, her prestige acquired at Munich would be lost. There remained nothing for it but to march into Prague.

The *coup* was carefully prepared. The Slovaks, subservient to German orders, were used as a pretext. The proclamation of Slovak independence was sure to provoke incidents which would provide a pretext for German intervention. Had the Slovak problem been the real issue, there would have been no reason for the Germans to march into Prague. But the aim, from the beginning, was to annex Czecho-Slovakia as a whole. In the Czech parts of the country the German troops came as conquerors, in the Slovak parts they were supposed to come as friends; but the result was the same.

The effects of the Czech tragedy can only be described as a serious check to the original Nazi conception of empire-building. In the country where the Nazis started with the greatest chances, they had been forced to abandon the idea of indirect rule through their friends in favour of ruthless conquest. That General Gajda, the Czech Fascist leader, is now proclaimed Führer of the Czechs at the point of German bayonets does not change the situation. This man had not been able to win a single seat in parliament for his party. Had the Germans ruled Czecho-Slovakia through Beran, there would have been no need for their direct interference. Their proclamation of Gajda is liable to ruin what little prestige Fascism has among the Czech people.

But the Czech problem cannot be understood as a local Czech affair only. Czech resistance to German claims, since January at least, was one element in a development concerning the whole south-east. Everywhere, in these regions, the German drive, as we shall see in the next chapter, had encountered serious resistance. Everywhere German prestige, which seemed so unchallenged after Munich, had suffered. Something very near an anti-German bloc was in the process of arising in the south-east. The German stroke at Prague was largely aimed at removing this threat, at restoring German prestige, and at launching a new German offensive in the whole area.

To a certain degree, Germany has attained these aims. But she has done so by changing her conception of imperialism in the wider area of the south-east, just as much as she had done in Czecho-Slovakia herself. The conquest of Prague, the encirclement of Poland from the south through Slovakia, the advance towards the Rumanian border have instilled fear into the Governments of all the south-eastern countries. So far Germany has been successful. But with fear goes hatred and a preparedness to resist if there is a chance. The Germans no longer come as friends. They are expected now to conquer and to oppress. In the whole south-east they have moved from a policy of indirect rule to one of main force.

CHAPTER IX

THE SOUTH-EAST: CONCLUSION

THE problems which brought about the downfall of Czecho-Slovakia are clearly outlined in all the other countries of the south-east. In all the countries between Hungary and Greece, the original German conception was one of indirect rule through close economic co-operation and through pro-German Governments and mass movements. In all these countries, however, German indirect rule meets with the most serious difficulties, and it is very doubtful whether Germany in the end will be able to do without direct conquest. It is equally doubtful whether she will be able to swallow as much as she needs in order to establish firmly her domination.

The case in many respects is much more difficult in most of the countries concerned than it was in Czecho-Slovakia. German methods of exploitation may be somewhat less ruthless in Yugoslavia or Greece than they were in Czecho-Slovakia, but then most of the Balkan countries control products absolutely indispensable to German rearmament, and she cannot treat them with much consideration. She must have her wheat, cotton, oil, antimony, bauxite, copper, lead, etc., and cannot pay for them adequately. In the case of Rumanian oil at least, German demands are absolutely essential for Germany's political intentions and she must try by every means to reduce Rumania to a state of complete economic subjection.

Yet while her economic needs are very urgent, her political sway over those countries is not assured. Czecho-Slovakia, after Munich, lay before Germany like a broken reed and yet attempted resistance. The other Balkan countries have means of resistance and are not ready to give up without at least some attempts at putting these means to use. It was a mistaken impression when, after Munich, the world believed that Germany would no longer find any resistance in the Balkans. It is true that no Balkan country could resist German armed intervention without the help of either the western powers or Soviet Russia. But as long as there is the slightest chance of such help forthcoming, none of the Balkan countries is likely simply to give in.

At present they are all playing for time, giving in to German demands, especially in the economic field, but at the same time trying to keep their independence and to wait for better times. It is very unlikely that this game can succeed in the long run in any of the Balkan countries. But it is not intended for the long run. If it fails, it will still have had the effect of forcing Germany away from her conception of indirect rule towards the exceedingly dangerous policy of direct conquest.

This whole game obviously makes part of the diplomatic battle between the great powers. And this diplomatic contest is increasingly conducted as a fight for position preliminary to the outbreak of actual hostilities. The power nearest to the spot is not even Germany but the Soviet Union. Russia, however, is interested only in the independence of her immediate neighbours, Poland, Rumania, and Turkey. Her interests hardly go beyond that modest aim. France, which after the War was paramount in that part of the world, has cleared out almost completely. England never had any very strong interests, except in Greece and Turkey, and if today she is widening the scope of her activity it is in view of the probability of more serious developments.

The power primarily interested in the Balkans was in fact Italy. Italy had fought the Great War largely in order to attain supremacy in the Balkans. She failed to reach that aim through the peace treaties. Under the Fascist regime she had again tried and had in spite of considerable resistance acquired a substantial amount of influence in all the countries concerned. Albania had become a *de facto* Italian protectorate and Italy's bridgehead in the Balkans long before Italy wantonly conquered her by main force. But the keystone of the Italian position was her alliance with Austria and Hungary, which from 1934 onwards had transformed these two countries into something very near Italian protectorates. Relations between Rome and Warsaw were decidedly good; Czecho-Slovakia could be trusted to be hostile to Germany. Thus Italy had succeeded in forming a complete barrier against German intrusion into the Balkans.

Germany was well aware why she encouraged Mussolini's Ethiopian adventure. While Mussolini conquered African mountains, which for many years to come must remain unprofitable, Germany concluded an alliance with Austria and at the same time broke into Italy's markets in the Balkans. Yugoslavia and Greece, especially, had been seriously hit by the sanctions, and Germany offered to buy the goods which they could no longer deliver to Italy, but on condition that she would receive a substantial share of their products. Ever since then the share of Italy in the Balkan trade has decreased and Germany's share has grown. The political effects have been equally important. It must be remembered that at least in Yugoslavia, Greece, and Turkey, Italy was extremely unpopular and that these countries were only too glad to find German support against Italian pressure.

It is an irony of fate that Italy concluded her alliance with Germany just at the moment when Germany was despoiling her. She had no choice, for the Ethiopian War had spoiled her relations with the west. And then Hitler saw to it that Italy involved herself in a new costly and unprofitable adventure in Spain while he himself invaded Austria and Czecho-Slovakia. This finally broke the Italian barrier against German penetration of the Balkans. The possibility of direct military intervention was now added to German political and economic influence. Today Germany takes more than forty per cent of Hungary's and Yugoslavia's trade, three and five times the trade of Italy with these countries. Before 1936 the German share in both countries was less than the Italian one. And the political balance in both countries has shifted even more strongly.

We cite these two countries merely as examples. Similar developments have taken place in the whole south-east. The chief effect of German-Italian co-operation was invariably the driving out of Italy. This applies not only to the Balkans. Beyond them lie the vast lands of the Near East, where Italy and Germany are attempting to uproot French and English influence. Whether they will succeed is another question. But in case of success, here too the major share will go to Germany.

The German Empire in the south-east is built upon the ruins of the would-be Italian Empire. It is an unexpected result of Mussolini's drive for Italian greatness. The Italians are a politically gifted people, and their average statesmen knew the art of getting considerable slices of territory through modesty and manœuvring. Not one of them would have conceived the idea that anything could be more important to Italy than her position in the eastern Mediterranean. It needed the would-be genius of Mussolini to throw all this away for the conquest of African mountain fastnesses and of an untenable position in Spain. Whatever Italy in the end will keep, she will now keep as a vassal of Germany.

Nowhere is this situation clearer than in Hungary, which from being most directly under Italy's influence has become the country most directly under German sway and this against all obvious interests of Hungary herself. As pointed out in an earlier chapter, the Hungarian claim for treaty revision is one of the chief elements of disturbance in that area and the one which lends itself most to foreign intervention. Of the regions Hungary lost through the War, Croatia, which is now Yugoslav, before the War had enjoyed home rule under Hungary. Hungary does not raise any claim to that area. A small German-speaking area on Hungary's western borders, the so-called Burgenland, was given to Austria at the peace conference and has since been greatly coveted by Hungary. But Hungarian claims for this territory were dropped when Hungary and Austria both came under Italian tutelage, and now when this region has become German, there is no longer any question of a revision in favour of Hungary.

Hungary, however, upholds all her other claims. She claims Slovakia and the Carpatho-Ukraine; she claims Transylvania from Rumania and the so-called Voivodina, a stretch of country on her southern borders, from Yugoslavia. But in respect to each of these claims she has a minimum and a maximum programme, the former on linguistic, the latter on historical grounds. Czecho-Slovakia, Rumania, and Yugoslavia acquired considerable compact Hungarian minorities through the peace treaties and it is these minorities which Hungary claims back in the first place. But the greater part of the territory ceded to these three countries was not Hungarian in language but Slovak, Ruthenian, Rumanian, and Serb. Only the upper classes in town and country were Hungarian. Yet Hungary claims these regions on the strength of the historical unity of the country under the crown of St. Stephen within the natural boundaries which she held for more than a thousand years. The claim is stronger in the case of Slovakia, the Carpatho-Ukraine, and the Voivodina than in the case of Transylvania, which had long enjoyed a sort of home rule under the Hungarian crown.

There is no absolute boundary line between the minimum and the maximum programme of revision. For this the linguistic boundaries are not nearly clear enough. The nationalities are intermingled and in some cases, e.g., in the Voivodina, to such an extent that it is impossible to say which area belongs to which. Besides, there are not only Hungarian minorities. Will the Germans in the Voivodina and in Transylvania go to Hungary, or to Yugoslavia and Rumania respectively? These German minorities, in case of treaty revision in that area, will act entirely upon orders from Berlin and can decide the issue.

But on the whole the German position is clear and is in absolute contradiction to the Italian view. Italy backs Hungary's historical claims, the claims for full restitution. Germany backs only her linguistic claims. The question for the first time came to a head after Munich, when Germany and Italy arbitrated between Hungary and Czecho-Slovakia. The German view obtained as against the view of Italy and Hungary, which was backed by Rumania and Poland. In accordance with the Nazi principle of "one language, one country," Hungary got back her minorities and nothing more, though Italy obtained for her a fairly broad interpretation of what actually was Hungarian-speaking country.

The German attitude is certainly not dogmatic. The Vienna award (the arbitration just mentioned) was dictated by a number of secondary considerations. Germany regarded Slovakia as her vassal whom she wanted to protect and the Carpatho-Ukraine as her spring-board against Poland. She wanted to prevent a common Polish-Hungarian border which would help to create a bloc of neutrals (Poland, Hungary, Rumania, with the possible adherence of the other Balkan countries) against the German advance. Finally, she wanted to punish the Hungarian Government for insufficient pliability to Nazi pressure.

But that did not prevent Germany from constantly fanning the flames in that part of the world. While organizing the Slovak and Ukrainian storm troops who defended their little countries against Hungary, she at the same time helped to bring under Nazi influence the Hungarian irregulars who constantly raided the border. The constant small warfare which is now raging in these regions is all to her advantage, and she has so far made no effort to discourage Hungary seriously in the pursuance of her wider aims. She had to give in to these Hungarian aspirations when on the day of the German entry into Prague the Hungarians marched into the Carpatho-Ukraine, broke up the Ukrainian nationalist movement in those parts, and established a common border with Poland, much against Germany's wish.

The Hungarian occupation of the Carpatho-Ukraine (or of Ruthenia, as it is now called again) is the first instance of Hungary's recovery of territory inhabited by non-Hungarians. The Germans certainly regard it as only a temporary settlement and expect to swallow all Hungary some day. Yet the results are serious. The Ukrainian nationalists feel themselves betrayed by Germany. As long as Germany seemed to stand by the principle of self-determination, she could be completely trusted by the oppressed nations of the southeast. Now the Ukrainians know that they are only a pawn in a game and would certainly be sacrificed in case of a German-Russian understanding. The Ukrainians, however, are one of the biggest problems of the south-east.

Stretching from the Carpatho-Ukraine over South-Eastern Poland and Southern Russia down to the Caucasus, they count at least forty million souls. Having no country of their own, they constitute the biggest unsolved national problem in Europe. Hitler and his Russian-born adviser on foreign affairs, Alfred Rosenberg, have consistently worked for a German protectorate over an independent Ukraine. It would give Germany control over one of the richest wheat-producing areas in the world, over the coal basin of the Donetz with all its in-dustries; it would cut off Russia from the Black Sea, so as to make her entirely powerless and unimportant. It would crush Poland by taking her in the rear. It would bring Germany so near the oil of Baku that she could hardly be prevented from taking it. It would bring her into dangerous proximity to India. German control of the Ukraine was one of the stipulations of the Treaty of Brest-Litovsk, forced upon the Bolsheviks in 1918.

A German-controlled Ukraine is the greatest dream of German imperialism in Europe. To it Hitler has had to sacrifice his co-opera-tion with the Russian nationalist émigrés, who do not want to give up an essential part of Russia. This co-operation could certainly be resumed at a later stage when the Ukraine would be independent and the Soviet regime would be broken. But at present Hitler rightly considers the potentialities of Ukrainian nationalism as being more important than the dreams of rootless Moscow refugees in Paris cafés. What the potentialities of Ukrainian nationalism really are, it is difficult to say. In Poland, they are certainly very great. There are about seven million Ukrainians living in Poland, more than ninety per cent of them poor tenant farmers under Polish landlords, so that social and national revolution in the Ukraine merge. The Poles have reacted against this danger with a regime of sanguinary terrorism which is among the worst in Europe, and their attempts at creating a pro-Polish movement in the Polish Ukraine have consistently failed.

It is more difficult, owing to the lack of any reliable information, to gauge the importance of Ukrainian nationalism in the Soviet

Ukraine. Two things are certain. The peasantry of the Soviet Ukraine was the richest and most property-minded of all Russia. They loathed collectivization of land, and hundreds of thousands of recalcitrant peasants from this area have been removed to die in Arctic concentration camps. At the same time the Soviets, in contrast to Poland, periodically made serious and successful efforts to create a Ukrainian-speaking upper class of political and factory officials, schoolteachers, etc., only to crush this same rising upper class when it started to show symptoms of Ukrainian nationalism. Terrific purges against Ukrainian nationalists within the Communist Party of the Soviet Ukraine date back to as early as 1928 and have never since ceased. There must be a lot of inflammable material in that part of the world. Everywhere else the nationalism of a rising intelligentsia has proved to be an important factor, but where, as in the Ukraine, it is combined with peasant unrest it is threatening indeed.

The whole problem could certainly become practical only in case of a war between Germany and the Soviet Union. In Russia, as little as in Germany, a rising from within, lacking substantial support from without, has small chance. And it is not likely that Germany will attack Soviet Russia so long as she can get rich booty elsewhere without war. In the meantime the Ukrainian movement remains a big asset to Germany in her game with Poland.

Now, to come back to our starting-point, this greatest dream of German expansion in Eurasia has been threatened and partly spoiled by the minor question of Hungarian revisionism. It is obvious that Germany cannot in the long run tolerate such a position. It is obvious, too, that the conflict between Germany and Hungary is inevitable. Hungary's historical claims clash with Germany's wider aims. In the meantime, it is true, Germany uses Hungary's historical claims for her own ends. Having been forced to accept some of these claims as a result of her rash march into Prague, Germany now encourages Hungary to raise these claims in full against Rumania. But Hungary, while accepting German backing, has so far refused to attack Rumania by main force.

The position would be different could Germany break up the Hungarian regime from within and install a Nazi regime in its stead. It seemed an easy task, and from month to month the world expected it to happen. After the occupation of Austria, Hungary was directly within reach of the German army, and it was almost certain that in case of a German attack, nobody would come to her help. In this situation Hungary had to make big concessions, had to join the anti-Comintern pact, to conclude trade agreements extremely favourable to Germany, and to dismiss her former Foreign Minister and replace him by a man more acceptable to Germany. Yet the final surrender did not take place. On the contrary, Hungary is thwarting Germany's Ukrainian plans.

The reason for this is that Germany's strong points in the Hungarian game are at the same time her weak spots. It would be all very well if Germany, in Hungary, could co-operate with the aristocracy and the business class connected with it. But the aristocracy has a proud tradition of independence and power which is incompatible with German aims, and the business class, even a small section of it which is not Jewish, is in despair over Germany's trade policy. Germany, by forcing her finished products upon Hungary, by forcing her to sell mainly to Germany on barter and thus depriving her of free exchange, stifles Hungarian industrial development. Since the big depression, Hungary has set out to supply her own industrial needs, and now Germany is attempting to throw her back to the status of a mainly agricultural country. It is a policy which must be welcome to the wheat-growing peasants who are, after all, the bulk of the nation, but not by far its most powerful section. Everybody else is antagonized.

In this situation, the Germans launched a real revolutionary movement, a movement for the expropriation of the large landowners by the peasants. It is a tendency deeply enough rooted in Hungarian history. And the Germans naturally couple the outcry for agrarian revolution with the traditional deep-rooted anti-Semitism of the Hungarians, giving it a particularly ferocious twist. Incidentally, anti-Semitism in Hungary is hardly less revolutionary than agrarian revolution. If the latter tends to destroy the landed aristocracy, the former aims a deadly blow at the bourgeoisie, which to a very large extent is Jewish. The Hungarian aristocrat traditionally dislikes the Jew, but after all there are many ties of blood and interest between the two groups.

The double battle-cry of agrarian revolution and anti-Semitism is apt to unite the peasant masses with the non-Jewish intelligentsia against the traditional ruling class of Hungary. But precisely for that reason it is a manoeuvre of dubious value. The Nazis cannot wish to unleash revolution in Hungary while keeping down the masses in Austria and Czecho-Slovakia. And at the same time their policy is likely to alienate the Hungarian aristocracy, which otherwise might be a natural ally. This aristocracy has stood many shocks. It has outlasted the Turks, the Habsburgs, and the Bolsheviks. It combines great shrewdness with esprit de corps and ruthlessness. The Germans have already had occasion to notice this.

Their conception was one of undermining the traditional ruling classes in Hungary by driving one Hungarian Government after another towards Nazism. Under mass pressure, subsequent Governments would be forced to adopt programmes increasingly near to the Nazi point of view, until no opposition to Nazism would be left. But so far, under incredibly difficult conditions, the Hungarian aristocracy has had the better of them. The fate of the Imredyi Government was characteristic in this respect. Imredyi suceeded Daranyi in May 1938, when, as a result of Germany's capture of Austria, Nazism in Hungary assumed dangerous proportions. At that time Imredyi was regarded as the strong man who would wipe out Nazism. But in the process of fighting against Nazi influence, he had to adopt a great deal of the Nazi programme, ending up with an attempt to create a totalitarian party in competition with the Nazis. Originally Imredyi had been Regent Horthy's man. But the moment Imredyi touched the traditional aristocratic parliamentarianism of Hungary and began seriously to tackle agrarian reform, he was no longer Horthy's man. All Hungary had paid lip service to Imredyi's programme, and it was his own programme which brought him down. Budapest, of course, had always known that he had a Jewish grandmother, but just for the fun of it, at the right moment, his adversaries discovered another Jewish ancestor of his about a hundred and thirty years back. This brought Imredyi down and had the additional advantage of holding up anti-Semitism to ridicule. A stout supporter of the aristocratic party, Count Teleki, succeeded him and the Nazis have to begin all over again.

It is quite conceivable that in its turn the Teleki Government may come closer to the German point of view, but it is equally conceivable that again a Jewish great-grandmother will turn up in time for one or another leading member of the Government. The Hungarian aristocracy has outwitted many adversaries. In the present circumstances this game can hardly continue indefinitely. But it is not likely to end sooner than Hungarian independence itself. And the Germans, should they finally conquer the country, will find it very difficult to rule it without its traditional upper class. This upper class, in its turn, looks down, as upon parvenus, upon the oldest aristocracies of Europe, and will not be ready simply to serve the Nazis. There could be no question of successful physical resistance against Germany on the part of Hungary. Yet the political problem of Hungary is a hard nut for the Nazis to crack.

The situation in Rumania has many features in common with that of Hungary, but there are outstanding differences too. Anti-Semitism is even more important in Rumania than in Hungary owing to the almost complete absence of a national Rumanian middle class. The sons of wealthy peasants who now, through the universities, make their way to lucrative careers find the Jews the chief obstacle in their path. It is only since the War that any real middle class has gradually emerged in Rumania out of these peasant elements, and it is altogether fiercely anti-Semitic. It is from these

elements that the pro-Nazi Iron Guard of Codreanu has been recruited. It certainly has the allegiance of a very considerable section
of the active youth.

But the point about Rumania is this, that the politically active section of the population is small. There is no very important peasant
unrest in Rumania, which carried out a substantial measure of
agrarian reform after the war. What peasant movement exists under
the leadership of M. Maniu belongs rather to the Left than to the
Right. The young Fascist intelligentsia in Rumania does not have
to fight against a ruling class with deeply rooted political traditions,
but it cannot count on fervent mass support as do the Hungarian
Nazis.

The upper classes, naturally, are outright anti-Nazis. The army,
which is traditionally pro-French and anti-German, the very influential Orthodox Church, the old-style politicians, and the Jewish
bourgeoisie form a bloc which it is almost impossible to destroy.
This bloc is quite able to beat the Nazis at their own game. Rumania
has a thorough strain of orientalism in its tradition, and torturing
and killing political adversaries were taught to the Rumanians by
the Turks long before there were Nazis.

In their own way the Rumanians have been completely successful
for almost a century. It is King Carol who is the embodiment of
their specific political tradition. Now that he feels himself threatened
by the Nazi advance, he is hampered in his actions neither by the
democratic qualms of the Czechs nor by the *point d'honneur* of the
Hungarian aristocracy. He simply fights back. It is a terrible thing
to say that the countries most successful in resisting Nazi methods
are those who have been least imbued with the decencies of western
civilization. It is a fact, however.

After Munich, King Carol came to London to ask for help. He
did not get all he wanted and went to Berchtesgaden to ask for a
compromise. Then Hitler thought that he had got him and appar-
ently King Carol did nothing to disillusion him. It so happened that
Codreanu and a number of his mates found themselves in prison

for a couple of murders they had committed with their own hands in the open street. Hitler expected to see Codreanu invested with power after his conversation with King Carol. But Rumania as a whole revised her ideas concerning pogroms after a fortnight's interlude of fierce anti-Semitism in February 1938 led to a complete stoppage of business. Since then Codreanu had been a good deal less popular, and Carol found himself strong enough to take stern measures. Codreanu and a considerable number of his followers were killed "while trying to escape."

The King, with the support of army and Church, has established a sort of totalitarian dictatorship of his own, wiping out the Rumanian Nazis. There was some commotion in the country but no serious sign of disintegration. Only the German minority, strictly organized on Nazi lines, remains a very serious problem.

There is no country like Rumania to prove that economic and political developments need not coincide. Rumanian oil is indispensable to Germany and she must get it by threats or inducements. At first Hitler had to take meekly the killing of his lieutenant Codreanu. The fact that Germany must at all costs remain on amicable terms with Rumania in order to get Rumanian oil did not in any way weaken Rumania's position. Almost immediately after the dramatic catastrophe of Rumanian Fascism, the Germans signed a new trade agreement. For years now they have taken twenty-five per cent of Rumanian oil.

Only after the collapse of Czecho-Slovakia did the situation change, and Germany by means of direct military threats forced a new trade agreement upon Rumania. Its provisions are far-reaching. Not only is the German share in Rumanian oil increased but the Rumanians grant the Germans the right of opening new wells with their own men and equipment. Rumania promises to develop both her mining industry and her agriculture on lines fitting into the German four-year plan. The effects remain to be seen. But the idea of Germany's getting political control over Rumania merely by economic penetration is somewhat too simple.

Hungary, in case of an international clash, may side with Germany. Rumania, despite the German economic penetration, will certainly be among her enemies, unless she is thrown to the wolves unsupported like Czecho-Slovakia.

The situation in Yugoslavia is much more complex, owing to the extreme complexity of the political structure of that country. Germany, both in the west of the country and on the Hungarian border, spends a lot of money on buying up land for German colonists, thus artifically creating a minority problem. German trade with Yugoslavia has been considerable, but there is no other country where it has led to so many conflicts, because of the classical German methods of running up a balance against themselves and then covering it by deliveries of inferior quality or utility. After Munich, Herr Funck, the present German Minister of Economics, offered Yugoslavia a trade agreement which would have fitted her into German rearmament plans, developing her production of raw materials at the expense of her industries. But this agreement was not ratified and conflicts continued about the operation of the narrower agreement in force.

As elsewhere, it is the political and not the economic aspect which finally decides. And here for many years the Germans backed the wrong horse, the extremely unpopular Government of Stoyadinovitch. Stoyadinovitch, an exponent of the army and a very strong Serbian centralist, found little support among his own Serbs and was fiercely hated by the Croats. Only the Mohammedans and the Slovenes gave him full support. But the Slovenes, who are strong Catholics and inhabit the westernmost part of Yugoslavia, grew increasingly wary about German pacific penetration. After all, the railway from German Vienna to Italian Trieste leads right across their territory. In case of war, the Axis would have to occupy that railway, and the Slovenes, inveterate enemies of the local Germans, could not expect mild treatment at the hands of Germany.

Thus even the Slovenes turned about, and their new policy is well in agreement with the feelings of the army, which is fiercely anti-

German by tradition. It was really the German threat that quite unexpectedly brought Stoyadinovitch down, though it would be a mistake to describe him as completely pro-German. The simple fact
about Stoyadinovitch was that, hated as he was by his people, he
could not afford to offend Germany.

At first his downfall was regarded as a considerable setback to
Germany. The Regent Prince Paul made known his intention to
construct a Government on a broader basis, including the Croats
after redressing their grievances against Serbian centralism. The
Serbs on the whole must be regarded as anti-German, but the bulk
of Croat opinion is not only anti-German but very strongly pro-
French and pro-British. Yet the fall of Stoyadinovitch was less of a
German defeat than appeared at first.

The Germans at that moment changed their game. They had
backed a weak and unpopular Government against the masses. They
now decided to permeate the mass movements themselves. The
Croats have generally shown as little desire to come to an understanding with the Serbs as the Serbs have shown to satisfy the grievances of the Croats. Germany is now setting out to give the Croatian
nationalist movement a twist in her own favour.

On the face of it it is not an easy task. There was a time when the
Croatian nationalists flirted with Moscow. They have always been
strongly democratic, and the claim for an end to the dictatorship
and for genuinely free elections has been their main plank since 1928.
Moreover, they are ardent Catholics. Yet deeply discredited as democracy is since Munich, everything is possible. No nationalist
movement in Eastern Europe puts democracy before its national
ideals. And if the Germans succeed in convincing the Croats that they
will help them, they will have won the race. They may then follow
a policy of making the Yugoslav Government bend to their wishes
by pressure from without and within while sowing discord and revolution inside Yugoslavia's borders. This new German policy has
much greater chances than the old one.

Yet difficulties may arise at a later stage. If one compares Poland,

Hungary, Rumania, and Yugoslavia, the German chances in these countries can be summed up as follows: Poland would be difficult to conquer and almost impossible to rule; Hungary would be easy to conquer but difficult to rule; Rumania would be difficult to conquer, but once conquered would probably be easily held with the help of the Iron Guard. Yugoslavia might be conquered with some difficulty, but that the proud Serbs and the wily Croats could ever abstain from a fierce vendetta against their German conquerors is almost inconceivable. Generally speaking, Germany must find it very difficult to rule over Slavs.

The position in Greece is still fairly similar to that which obtained in Yugoslavia before the fall of Stoyadinovitch. Here too the Germans are backing a weak and unpopular Government which is dependent on their support precisely because of its weakness. There is this difference between Stoyadinovitch and the Greek dictator, General Metaxas, that the latter is pro-German, not out of opportunity, but out of deep conviction. He is German-trained, and while the Yugoslavs always tried to keep up a simulacrum of parliamentarianism, Metaxas is toying with the idea of a totalitarian party ruling the country under his leadership. But so far nothing much has come of these plans. It is still simply the rule of the army which obtains in Greece, with almost all the people hostile to it.

Germany won hegemony in Greece owing to many reasons. The country is traditionally anti-Italian and pro-British, but Metaxas is anti-British too. Thus Germany was really his only choice. Economically the Germans got ahead of Italy during the period of sanctions and have kept a firm grip ever since. But in Greece, which must import most of her food, the scarcity of free exchange which results from bartering with Germany is a particularly serious problem.

There is one aspect of the Greek situation, however, where Germany's position is really splendid. This is the direct German intrusion in Greek administration. Everywhere in the Balkans, Germany makes big efforts to obtain key positions for German agents. But in most countries German methods are only indirect. What key positions the Germans acquire are mostly connected with economic activities. Officers and engineers concerned with armament deliveries, with the creation of industrial centres, and with town-planning must obviously know a great deal about the vital spots of the countries where they work. But in Greece the German personnel plays a larger part. There, as in Bulgaria and in Spain, the Gestapo quite openly maintain her officers, and Germans hold important positions in the State administration. Even so, the attitude of Greece, in case of an international clash, cannot be regarded as certain. It has been seen that foreign advisers in a country have been got rid of at the last moment. The English naval mission to Constantinople before the War, which did not prevent Turkey from joining the other side, is one notable instance.

Of all the countries of the south-east, Bulgaria is the smallest (next to Albania) and the one most directly under German influence. Germany took more than sixty per cent of her trade in 1938 and may take anything up to eighty per cent in 1939. All Balkan currencies are to a large extent dependent on the whims of the Reichsbank, but it could be said of Bulgaria that her currency is actually managed from Berlin. Bulgaria has no strong desire to become industrialized. Being mainly a peasant country, with exceedingly modest requirements, her economic interests clash less with those of Germany than is the case with any other Balkan country. The rule of the Germans in her economic life and administration is great indeed.

Politically the position of Bulgaria differs from that of all of her neighbours in so far as she ranks among the defeated of the Great War and therefore favours treaty revision. All the other Balkan countries would certainly prefer neutrality to any other policy, and this desire is embodied in the Balkan Pact between Turkey, Greece, Rumania, and Yugoslavia. The pacific intentions of Bulgaria are not so certain. To this day she has refused to sign the Balkan Pact, though she has constantly moved nearer to the signatories since

1934. Yet her aspirations for treaty revision have not died. The German conflict with Rumania in particular has revived Bulgarian hopes for recovery of the territory lost to that country.

As in so many other cases, here again Germany's assets are at the same time her weak spots. Bulgaria's desire for treaty revision certainly works in favour of Germany. But German backing of Bulgarian nationalism is bound to raise the suspicions of all those who want to get rid, once and for all, of the past and its conflicts. Now such a desire to break completely with the past is the very essence of the policy of the present Bulgarian Government. Here international and national questions are inextricably intertwined.

Bulgaria's chief quarrel was not with Rumania but with Yugoslavia for Macedonia. For more than ten years, from June 1923 to May 1934, the armed gangs of Macedonian refugees terrorized every Bulgarian Government, threatening disaster if Bulgaria came to a sincere understanding with Yugoslavia. At times, the Macedonians were the real masters of the country, and it was mainly owing to their internal splits that their influence later declined. In 1923 Professor Zankov overthrew the peasant Government of Stambuliski with the help of the Macedonians and attempted to create a sort of Fascist dictatorship. He failed and the country returned after a time to a half-hearted sort of democracy.

Then, in 1934, the military *coup* of General Georghiev overthrew democratic government. But this time the Macedonians did not gain from the rising. On the contrary, the new Government was determined to make an end of their tyranny and wiped them out in just retribution for their unspeakable murders and atrocities. Ever since, the relations between Belgrade and Sofia have been decidedly good. The military dictatorship of Georghiev after a time gave place to the administrative dictatorship of Kiosse-Ivanov. Under him Bulgaria's foreign policy remained unaggressive and the regime grew decidedly milder. Kiosse-Ivanov is an old diplomatist not given to harsh methods, and he has most definitely the backing of the King.

The political position in Bulgaria, therefore, is this: very considerable masses unflinchingly stick to the peasant party in spite of its official dissolution. It is a mass movement of the Left. On the other hand there are the Fascist groups whose most outstanding leader is Professor Zankov. They are exceedingly pro-German and clamour for a more active policy in the matter of treaty revision. But their influence has been weakened by the destruction of the Macedonians, and their chief following now is university students and similar groups, not a negligible quantity in a country such as Bulgaria. The Government which, like most Balkan dictatorships, has no very strong following of its own, rejects both their bellicose intentions and their Fascist views. While constantly drawing closer to the Balkan Pact, it at the same time undertakes a policy of return to normality at home, including even a measure of parliamentary control. In these conditions it would certainly be a mistake to describe Kiosse-Ivanov as a German agent. Even in case of an international conflict Bulgaria would probably attempt to sell her neutrality at a high price rather than share in the fighting.

An attempt at summing up the situation in the whole of Eastern Europe might lead to the following conclusions: the dictatorships which rule everywhere from Estonia to Greece are invariably weak and in many cases actually tottering. Almost everywhere they are threatened by mass movements of the Left and of the Right. But the chances of the pro-Fascist elements' getting the upper hand merely by their own forces are everywhere very doubtful, and the very extremism of the Fascists makes it more doubtful whether they can get command without the use of main force. Besides, there are countries without any strong Fascist movement, such as Greece, Yugoslavia, and the Baltic countries. There are others such as Poland where a Fascist conquest would not favour Germany. The anti-German trends are of the most various kinds, but there is no country where they are not strong. German preponderance in those parts was mainly due to the absence of any serious countermove on the part of the other great powers, and even so is not assured in war. As soon as the influence of any other great power is felt in those regions, resistance against Germany grows to such an extent as to threaten her sway. It is therefore likely that in many cases the German policy of indirect penetration will fail and that the Germans will be driven to the use of main force, thus accelerating the mad drive towards an international clash. There is obviously little doubt that Germany could occupy much of the area concerned by main force at any time she chooses.

But it is precisely this possibility of an occupation by main force which raises the basic issue. Granted that Germany would be able to hold what she conquered, what would these possessions mean to her? The population of these regions is mostly Slavonic in language and almost everywhere near to the racial and psychological type of the Slavs. The Germans traditionally despise the Slavs (whom did they ever not despise?). But the birth-rate of the Slavonic peoples is much higher than that of Germany, their vitality is enormous, and their hatred of the Germans very deep-seated. The Nazi regime itself excludes every possibility of a conciliation. It has been found difficult for an empire to rule in the long run even old races such as the Indians and the Egyptians. But how, in the long run, an empire would be able to rule young, vital, rising people without any attempt at merging the conquerors and the conquered is a riddle which the wise men of racialism must be best able to solve.

There is one country in that region which remains completely outside all these considerations: Turkey. The Turkish dictatorship is not weak, but extremely strong. Its structure is similar in certain respects to that of the German regime. Opposition parties in Turkey have been not only formally dissolved and driven underground; actually they no longer exist. There is very little political life in the proper sense of the word in the country, and no power can hope to win influence in Turkey by bringing pressure from within to bear upon the Government. There are only two ways of winning Turkey. The one would be an attempt at direct conquest, and that for a great many reasons would be an exceedingly risky affair. The other is to convince the Government as it is of the usefulness of German friendship.

In Turkey, more clearly than in other countries, the importance of the political as against the economic factor can be understood. The type of trade between Turkey and Germany does not essentially differ from that between Germany and many other countries. Germany stands at the top of the list for Turkish exports and imports. Turkey has experienced the same difficulties with German trade methods as other countries. But the political effects have been totally different.

In a way Germany has been quite successful in gaining Turkish friendship. But this friendship does not go further than the strictest maintenance of Turkish independence allows. Turkey economically and politically profits from the present international tension. Being a strong power, she is wooed by Germany, Russia, and Britain. Besides constant economic help from Russia at practically no cost to herself, she has got quite a favourable trade agreement with Germany and at the same time accepted a British loan to the amount of £16,000,000. Germany tried in vain to drive out British competition in this field. After Munich, Germany granted £10,000,000 of so-called credits which are really German industrial deliveries to be spread over ten years in exchange for Turkish goods. But these much-advertised credits are in reality not much more than a rearrangement of former German contracts. Turkey does not want to become dependent upon Germany.

For this there is a definite reason: Turkey is the lucky, or as the case may be the unlucky, possessor of the Straits, which are a strategic crossroads of the first order. The Straits constitute the easiest access from the west and from India to Russia. Their closure decided the collapse of Russia during the last war. It is a foremost British as well as Russian concern to keep them open. And this interest coincides with the Turkish desire to keep the Straits open except when the Turks themselves wish to close them.

Germany, however, must desire to close the Straits at all costs in case of war, even if either Russia or Britain remained neutral, in order to prevent as much as possible any collaboration between these two powers. Turkey is therefore rightly afraid of a German breach of her neutrality in case of war and has shown great eagerness to join in some arrangement of collective security which would guarantee her complete dominion over the Straits.

But this is by no means the whole story. German periodicals and newspapers today quite openly revive the old Berlin-Baghdad idea, the idea of the German penetration of the Near and Middle East, with India as the final goal. The oil fields of Mosul and of Iran are alluring bounties. Germany today is carrying out a big propaganda campaign in Iraq as well as in all other Arabic-speaking countries. In Iran she already holds second place in exports and imports (the first place is held by the Soviet Union) and is developing Iranian basic industries and civil aviation. It must not be forgotten that in all these attempts Germany only returns to the old dreams of the War days.

These plans are not yet very much emphasized, but there is little doubt that in a way all Germany's campaigns in the south-east are only a vanguard encounter on her march towards Asia. The British Empire is unanimously proclaimed decadent by the foremost military theorists of Germany. The inference that Germany aims at striking at its most important link would be obvious even without the precedent of German action in Turkey, Iran, and Afghanistan.

Germany cannot contemplate naval action in those parts. She can only, as we shall see in the next chapter, attempt to cut British sea-routes to India by an attack by land. For her own advance she must rely on land-routes, thus reviving an old Napoleonic idea. There are two main land-routes to India. Both lead through Iran, the one on the northern shores of the Black Sea through the Ukraine, the other one along its southern shores through Turkey. If Germany wants to strike seriously in the Middle East, as she undoubtedly does, she must make Turkey her vassal. Action with the Ukraine as her only basis could not be effective. Turkey willingly fitted herself into that role in

1914. But the Turkey of 1939 is a different country. She does not want to be a vassal of any power. The strategic importance of the country is so great that she can expect support in case of an attack. And unlike the Balkan countries she has every means of defending herself. The fight for Turkey will largely decide the fate of the new German Empire.

CHAPTER X

AFRICA AND THE MEDITERRANEAN

WITH Africa we reach the sphere of German colonial claims proper. In Africa, Germany to a large extent uses methods different from those applied in other parts of the world. There from the outset she renounces methods of peaceful penetration and is openly out for territorial expansion. But that is not to say that the German approach to African problems is different in all respects from what we have so far described in relation to other parts of the world. In Africa, as elsewhere, we must consider two different aspects: Germany's immediate territorial expansion and the indirect aims connected with it.

So far Germany has raised clearly defined claims only to her former African colonies, and claims of a less precise sort for a share in the colonial possessions of the world. But these definite claims, here as in other cases, give access to much wider ends. The main problem for Germany, as we are going to show, is not to acquire this or that stretch of African jungle or desert but to get domination of the two main sea-routes between Europe and the East—the Mediterranean and the Cape. It is therefore impossible to separate the problems of Africa proper from the problems of the Mediterranean. Egypt and Palestine, Spain and the Spanish zone in Morocco, must be treated under one heading.

But let us first consider the German colonial claims proper. German colonial possessions before the War lay partly in the Pacific, and partly in Africa. The German case for the return of her former colonies is essentially built upon the contention that she was unlawfully deprived of them at the peace conference. It is noteworthy in this context that no serious claims have ever been raised for the return of the German colonies in the Pacific. There are many signs that Germany views Japan as the second great world power which is to remain after the expected crash of all the older empires. And the

136

Pacific is regarded as a Japanese zone of influence. It is perhaps amusing to speculate that if German dreams came true India would inevitably become an object of contention between Germany and Japan. At any rate, Germany is making serious efforts to win over sections of the Indian Nationalist movement. But beyond Calcutta there is no sign of German interference. This part of the world is regarded as a Japanese preserve.

If this factual renunciation of her Pacific claims weakens Germany's legal and moral case for the return of her old colonies, there still remains the economic case. For a long time Germany maintained that she needed colonies in order to settle her surplus population. It always was a specious claim because Germany's African colonies could not in any case take any substantial number of whites. In the meantime the Nazis, while claiming colonies on the ground of the overpopulation of Germany, are themselves increasing that overpopulation by their drive to raise the birth-rate.

But the decisive fact is obviously that all the talk about overpopulation has become obsolete. That argument could impress people while Germany had eight million unemployed. It is meaningless today when Germany is suffering from an acute shortage of labour. This shortage is bound to increase apace with the expansion of the German Empire. More and more men will be needed to rule subject countries, and less and less will be available for productive work in Germany itself. If the German attempt at empire-building succeeded, the Germans as a whole would become increasingly a race of rulers, leaving the heavier and more subordinate tasks to their subject races.

In the meantime Germany makes attempts to rally to her colonial claims countries which she hopes will one day become her vassals, such as Poland. The hope held out to smaller nations for a share in the German colonial empire is one more method of German indirect penetration in the countries concerned.

If the talk about overpopulation is of no value at all, the same thing cannot be said about the value of the former German colonies as producers of raw materials. It is not that Germany could get any essential raw materials out of her four former African colonies (Tanganyika, South-West Africa, Cameroons, and Togoland), or for that matter out of her former Pacific colonies. The most important raw material that she could get would be vegetable oils (twenty-three per cent of German imports are produced in former German colonies) and sisal, which is produced in Tanganyika in much greater quantities than Germany needs. Even at present, Germany imports these goods from her former colonies, thus taking about forty per cent of the exports of Tanganyika and of the Cameroons and more than eighty per cent of those of Togoland. But all this does not account for much in the German trade balance.

The real advantage to Germany would not lie in the supplies she could herself receive from her former colonies but in the exports of these colonies to third countries through which Germany might, once she owned them, acquire free exchange. This would be a definite advantage. The total exports of all the former German colonies amount to something like 156,000,000 marks. But of them a considerable part must be accounted to the exports of her Pacific colonies (especially the phosphate exports from the British mandate of Nauru). The rest must be balanced against imports to the colonies, and the balance cannot by any means become considerable. Germany maintains that she would develop the natural resources of her former colonies extensively but this is a doubtful proposition in view of her own industrial difficulties. Yet some items of the production of this region, such as South-West African diamonds, would undoubtedly constitute valuable assets for Germany.

Before the War, Germany's colonies were generally regarded as hardly worth having, and the costs of administration and economic development were much higher than any political or commercial advantages they might provide could possibly warrant. In spite of all the colonial propaganda on the part of Germany, it is very doubtful whether the situation would now be different. It is certain that Germany regards her colonial claims, like all her other present claims, only as stepping-stones to something else.

This "something else" might be the acquisition of a wider colonial area. Germany may hope to be able in an international crisis to raise gradually her colonial claims until they cover territory which never belonged to Germany, such as the Belgian Congo or some former Portuguese colonies. This again would be in keeping with German pre-War policy. The German conquest might be covered by some scheme of co-operation between all colonial powers, though it is very doubtful whether Germany would regard such a scheme as more than a plausible propaganda argument. In the end Germany probably would not accept anything but full sovereignty over any colonial territory she might acquire.

Vague as these larger German claims are at present, it is impossible to say anything definite about the value such wider conquests could have for Germany. They would probably at least supply her with a not unimportant amount of rubber, one of her basic raw materials for rearmament, and would generally tend to improve considerably her trade balance. But the decisive elements for the acquisition of self-sufficiency do not lie in Africa. Oil is to be had in Rumania, Mosul, and Persia, iron in Sweden, Lorraine, and Spain, foodstuffs and many minerals in the south-east. Tin and nickel could not be found in sufficient quantities either in Europe or in Africa. The economic value of any African colonies to Germany is therefore doubtful, and their value in case of war would entirely depend upon the domination of the seas.

Whatever economic value it promises, there is a specific psychological element involved in any German domination in Africa. The Nazi regime could not subsist if all its subjects were Nordics or reputed to be so. It can keep up its specific psychological appeal only by opposing the superior race of light to the inferior races of darkness. This, strange as it may seem, is an essential element of Nazism. So far the Jew has been the scapegoat, but the psychological value of the Jew for the Nazi regime is rapidly decreasing. The Jews are driven out. At the same time anti-Semitic propaganda in Germany has obviously overreached itself; the margin between the alleged power and dangerousness of the Jews and their misery is really too great. And finally, eighty million people oppressing half a million or one million really cannot provide the desired feeling of superiority.

The Slavs could not be used as substitutes for the Jews, for, however much the Slavs are despised by the Germans, Germany cannot waive all attempts to make them willing subjects of the German Empire. But the black race would provide an excellent substitute. Black skin is even better than black hair. The Negroes are most emphatically described as an inferior race in Germany; the equality granted to them in France and the participation of black troops in the occupation of the Rhineland are standard subjects of anti-French education in Germany. The black race is on the whole not sufficiently developed politically to need much consideration. Germany in Africa need not make, and if she gets a chance will not make, any attempts at indirect rule. Moreover, the Negroes are numerous enough to give the Germans the feeling of really being a superior race, ruling over hosts of sub-men.

Official publications in Germany proclaim that the blacks ought not to be admitted to any more highly skilled work, ought to be given no education or only a minimum amount of it, and that their religious life should be subject to special restrictions. The German idea of the black people is that they ought to be kept in a sort of collective slavery as against the slavery under individual owners to which they were subjected before the age of liberalism. This, however, is not incompatible with German propagandists' being interested in the movements of the natives in South Africa.

The psychological aspect is certainly not the basic one at present, though in the long run it may be very important indeed. But as things are, Germany has no chance of acquiring at once a very wide African empire. She might get back her colonies and even something more in an attempt at conciliation, provided she can convince the older colonial powers that she will then be satisfied. But she cannot by any means make wide conquests in Africa so long as she has not defeated Britain and France. The way to an African empire leads through victory in Europe. And the practically decisive problem, therefore, is not at all what value any African colonies might have for a well-established German empire, but what value her former colonies could have for her in case of an international conflagration. Here we return at once to a well-known field and well-known methods. As in other cases, so in the case of her African colonies, Germany's territorial claims are not an end in themselves but intended to give access to wider aims.

Germany's most important goal is undoubtedly the Union of South Africa, even though it is a goal never yet openly mentioned in German propaganda. South African politicians themselves are well aware of the threat. The importance of the Union for Germany is obvious and manifold. The Union dominates one of two sea-routes to India and probably the essential one in case of war, as the Mediterranean will be closed in case Italy joins the German side. The Union is the greatest gold-producer in the world. As it is doubtful whether the United States, in the next war, will deliver armaments on credit, cash in case of war will be nearly all-decisive. If Britain could not dispose of South African gold, she would find very great difficulties in meeting her needs. Germany, by gaining control of South African gold, would at one stroke get rid of all the limitations imposed upon her by the lack of free exchange. The other assets of the Union, such as her wool and her diamonds, would be fine acquisitions into the bargain.

The Union has only one and a half million white inhabitants, and towards them Germany can use all the methods she uses towards other white communities. The small number of whites spread over a very wide territory makes the attempt rather easier. As long as she does not rule the seas, she could never hope to conquer South Africa by force alone. But she can hope to conquer it by her usual methods, a combination of working from within and threatening from without. In this scheme the former German colonies, once returned to Germany, would play an important part.

It is not likely that Fascism in the precise meaning of the term could have much chance in South Africa. The strong Calvinist tradition of the Afrikander community on the one hand, and the economic stability of the Union on the other, are serious obstacles. It is true that, as against the safe position of business in the Union, there stands the poor white problem. The poor whites in the towns, and certain farmer elements suffering from all sorts of difficulties in the countryside, would provide an almost ideal recruiting field for a Fascist movement. But there is lacking in South Africa that broad stratum of frightened bourgeoisie and a despairing proletariat which in Germany and Italy received the Fascists as saviours.

Yet if Fascism in the proper sense of the word is unlikely, there exist sufficient elements in the political structure of the Union to bring about moves favourable to Germany and unfavourable to the British connexion. There are at least three major elements which may work in such a direction. There is, first, anti-Semitism, a very serious matter in South Africa, and a sort of prolongation and exacerbation of the hatred of the poor Boer farmer for the rich un-Calvinist bourgeoisie of the Rand. There is, second, the native problem, most important among all political problems of the Union. Here, it is well known, the British and the South African views diverge, the British view being dictated by humanitarian considerations and the South African one by the Rand's policy of cheap labour and the slave-owning traditions of the Boer community. It is true that outside the three British protectorates in South Africa, the Union can deal with its natives as it likes. Yet the affinity of the Union view in this matter to the German view is much closer than to the British. It is a matter where South African opinion is extremely sensitive. Anti-Semitism and resistance to the rise of the Negro merge together into something very near a German racial point of view.

These problems, finally, play their part in the controversy around the Afrikander extremists, the "nationalists" or Malanite Party. A few years ago it seemed that the old controversy between the British and the Afrikander community would come to rest, with only a small and decreasing minority of the Boers remaining outside the fold of the United South African Party, where British and Afrikanders co-operate. But things have taken another turn and Malanite influence is undoubtedly growing. Its strength in the country at present is certainly greater than its strength in parliament and there is no doubt that the recent centenary of Dingaan's Day (the victory of the Boer trekkers over the Zulus) has given it a new impulse. The Malanite movement grows on hostility to the Jews, the Negroes, and the British at one and the same time, however strange this proximity may be.

As usual, the growth of the extremists makes the moderates hesitate in their course. The controversies about the celebrations of Dingaan's Day, with the refusal to play the British national anthem, have shown that a current of separatist opinion exists even outside the Malanite fold. South Africa has this in common with Ireland: it has always been a dominion with a non-Anglo-Saxon majority. And if the British element is stronger in the Union than in Ireland, the feelings of at least one section of the non-British element need not be very different in both cases. The international implications, however, are quite different. A free Ireland is not very likely to turn pro-German. There is little doubt about the German sympathies of the Malanites.

These trends are serious enough, but it is not likely that any of them could come to a head in time of peace. In time of war, it would be quite a different matter. Most probably there will be no repetition of the Boer rising of 1914. But there may be a much more serious separatist political movement. It all depends on the fate of Tanganyika.

The Germans have their finger in the pie, first of all in the general line of anti-Semitism, race propaganda, and anti-British policy, but in addition in three definite respects. There is first the German colony in South-West Africa. This colony, though only a few tens of thousands strong, attempts to play the role of a real Henlein party in South Africa. On the one hand it claims the right of secession to Germany; on the other hand it works as a spearhead for all anti-

British tendencies. Agitation has grown so bad that special police measures had recently to be taken. Second, there is the German claim for colonies which may in many ways threaten South Africa, directly and indirectly. This threat, as usual, brings about attempts at conciliation as well as attempts at resistance. There are elements in the Union, best represented by Pirow, the War Minister, who would not at all like the Germans to come too close to the Union and just for that reason would prefer a policy agreeable to German wishes; witness Pirow's recent journey through Europe and his visit to Hitler.

Finally, and chiefly, there is, just as everywhere in Europe, the threat of the German bombers. This threat at present is non-operative, and as long as it does not actually operate all other German moves must be regarded as not very dangerous in themselves. But if Germany got back even the single colony of Tanganyika, Johannesburg would be within easy bombing range of the German air force. Without ever actually becoming a reality, this threat might completely upset the political balance. The small white communities outside Europe and America are all out for protection, and the British navy is the most powerful means of protection for them all. But the British navy would be no protection against German bombers. If Tanganyika became German again, the Union would have to take very strong and expensive protective measures of her own and might in the end be forced to fight a destructive war which would certainly not rouse the enthusiasm of the Afrikander community. Under such circumstances the separatist movement might become dangerous.

It is perhaps interesting to note that in South Africa, even more than elsewhere, Germany's economic action is entirely subsidiary to her political one. Germany has concluded a barter agreement for wool which as usual benefits the section most friendly to Germany, in this case the Boer farmers. But if it were only for that, the problem would not be very serious.

Thus the German conception of the conquest of Africa takes

shape. Germany, through a protectorate over a South African Union entirely dominated by the Afrikander element, to the exclusion of everything British, might rule the whole southern part of the continent and keep down the natives: this is the essential plan. Again such a plan may seem fantastic. But there are no German plans which are not fantastic. Germany's approach to the African problem is identical with her approach to all other problems. Her scheme is one of conquest by political means with little or no use of arms. If it succeeded, it would break the backbone of the British Empire. But given the geographical distances on the one hand, and the immediate British interests involved on the other, her chances of success are certainly very doubtful. She will try, however.

And it is not only in the southern half of the continent that she will try. The northern half is at least as important. But in the north there is no white community such as the Afrikanders on which to place her hopes. And incapable as Germany is of direct conquest, she must rely in certain respects, at least, upon her action in the mother countries. This at least applies to the Guinea Coast. Farther north the situation is again different.

On the Guinea Coast the German claims at present appear as almost subsidiary to those of Italy. We have dealt with the position in these parts already, indirectly, when we discussed the position of Alsace. The juxtaposition of Alsace, the Cameroons, and Togoland may seem strange and would in fact be meaningless if German expansion were an affair of military conquest. But the political aspect is altogether decisive. And Alsace has this in common with Togoland and the Cameroons, that they are territories which Germany may claim back from France. The settlement between France and Germany, in its turn, is not an isolated matter. It is one and the same problem as the settlement of the French-Italian antagonism. If France, under German pressure, would give up Tunis and Djibouti and renounce the integrity of her possessions, Germany would certainly get the French mandates into the bargain, at the moment of the collapse of French resistance. And if French resistance once collapsed, it would certainly not be a matter of the former German colonies only, but of all French West Africa.

Besides, the problems of the Guinea Coast are inseparable from the problems of North Africa, because the whole conflict centres in the Italian demands for Tunis, if for no other reason. And in North Africa, Italian help for German plans can be more direct, and Germany in North Africa is not even limited to Italian support. There is Nationalist Spain and there is the Arab nationalist movement.

On the surface it may seem as if in North Africa it were not a question of Italian support for Germany but of German support for Italy. The Mediterranean, and especially North Africa, seem to be a preserve of Italian expansion. But this would be underestimating the German capacity for expansion.

A look into any German newspaper is sufficient to convince one that Germany is at least as interested as Italy in the Palestinian troubles. Anti-Semitism provides an easy link between Germany and the Arab extremists. More likely than not, Italy has recently adopted anti-Semitism partly in order not to lose the race for popularity among the Arabs. Already, in this matter of anti-Semitism, Italy appears in the wake of Germany, even in North Africa and the Near East. Moreover, Italy has a very bad record with her own Arabs in Libya, whereas Germany's record is clean. Germany in Palestine, at least, can work through a German minority.

German action in the Arab world, moreover, is not entirely limited to Palestine. Leading men of the German regime have been keen about keeping in close contact with the Arab leaders and rulers. As early as December 1937 Herr von Schirach visited Damascus and Baghdad as well as Teheran and Ankara. A special department for the Near East exists in the German Ministry for Propaganda under the head of a certain Dr. Rudiger. Germany has opened diplomatic relations with Saudi Arabia and very strongly emphasized the fact. Finally, she does everything in her power to strengthen her position in Egypt, where she holds second place in imports and exports and provides important industrial plant.

The German game in these parts of the world is perhaps less obvious than elsewhere, but they are certainly not neglected. In Egypt, too, the more extreme forms of nationalism may be an asset to Germany, and much more so than to Italy, because the proximity of Libya does not make for Italian popularity. There are persistent rumours of German motorized divisions being specially trained for desert warfare, and of the presence of German troops in Libya. The threat to Suez is quite unmistakable, but the German-Italian competition is no less evident in these parts. If Germany has prevailed upon her Axis partner to give her a direct share in her actions in the eastern Mediterranean, it is doubtful whether Mussolini gave his assent very willingly. In substance, Germany in the Arab world is repeating the game she played with Italy in the Balkans. If she has no aspirations in Tunisia, and none perhaps in Algiers, she certainly has in the countries around the Suez Canal and the Red Sea.

This allows us to define more clearly the position Italy would have within a German Empire. It would not differ essentially from that of many other peoples. It would not be similar to that of Japan. At present, at least, Germany treats Japan as her only equal, a country whose interests she respects and whose zones of influence she avoids touching. In the case of Italy, the aim of German policy is, on the contrary, to bring her into as complete a dependence as possible. The Italians, once the German Empire was complete, would play a not very different part from that of other nations within it. The method of ruling might be considerably more indirect than in other cases, and Italy might enjoy a privileged position among Germany's vassal countries. But Germany, even now, does not treat Italy as a real equal, and has no intention of allowing her to follow an independent policy. Even at this early stage, Germany sees to it that Italy will not have any important zones of influence of her own, free from German interference. Germany has driven Italy out of the Balkans, is gradually getting hold of precisely that Arab national-ist movement which otherwise might be the spearhead of Italian expansion, and at the same time proves herself to be a very success-ful competitor of Italy in Spain. Thus, while Mussolini dreams of a Mediterranean Empire of his own, he is in fact helping to create Germany's Mediterranean Empire, both in the eastern and in the western Mediterranean. Already his liberty of movement is restricted. It would vanish completely once Germany had reached all her aims in Europe. In the case of Italy, as in any other case, German control, once established, would rapidly move towards an ever more ruthless form of domination.

It is true that at present the Germans still emphasize their modera-tion in all Mediterranean affairs. As in the case of the Arab national-ist movement, so in the case of Spain, they have contrived to appear as true friends, where Italy appears as a potential conqueror. That is precisely the German way of squeezing out the Italians. Whereas Italy acquired a considerable amount of unpopularity in Spain, by giving a considerable amount of support to the Nationalists, Ger-many, with much more limited help, and much greater restraint, has acquired great influence and popularity. Already the major share of Spain's iron-ore exports goes to Germany. And it is at least con-ceivable that British and French efforts to remove the Italians from Spain will in the end benefit the Germans.

There are obvious reasons why Germany must tread her way care-fully in Spain. General Franco is so much wooed on all sides at pres-ent as to be quite independent of German support, and the geo-graphic conditions exclude any possibility of direct German inter-ference except with the consent of France. On the other hand, the assets to be gained by Germany are enormous. The Spanish zone in Morocco is one strategic base for the starting of a Mohammedan re-volt against France, and if Germany wields more influence than Italy with Franco, her influence in the Mohammedan world in the western Mediterranean will be all the greater for it. German designs upon Morocco are again only a repetition of moves made before the

War. Then there are the Canaries, invaluable as a naval and air base, threatening Britain's Atlantic sea-route to India and lying within bombing distance of Brazil. Finally, there is Spain's prestige in South America, and if German influence on that continent works in close conjunction with Nationalist Spanish influence, the effects must be considerable indeed.

In Spain, as elsewhere, German success or failure depends finally upon the issue between the political forces within Spain, meaning by that, not the issue between the Republicans and Nationalists which is settled already, but the one between Monarchists and Fascists within the Nationalist camp. Formerly in Nationalist Spain there existed only one party, but in fact this party is divided into two strongly opposed wings. The Fascists in Spain already look much more to Germany than to Italy for guidance. It is true that a large part of the army, and the Church, the aristocracy, the civil service are Monarchist, and the Fascists at present have hardly a chance of complete success. But this might change once Germany were able to hold out to Spain serious prospects of territorial aggrandizement in Morocco or elsewhere. Spain, like Italy, might become a favoured nation under the German Empire, with colonial possessions of her own, but under strict German control. In the meantime the vision of a new Spanish Empire might tip the balance inside Spain in favour of the pro-German Fascist forces. They would certainly get the upper hand once Spain believed that there was no other master in Europe but Germany.

CHAPTER XI

LATIN AMERICA

THERE is no other instance so suggestive of the unlimited character of German expansion as Germany's penetration of South America. Germany obviously wants to trade with the South American countries and wants to trade with them advantageously. The Latin American countries in their turn have almost all been severely hit in their economic life for various reasons and are eager to find an outlet for their surplus products in the German market. The lack of foreign exchange makes every commercial transaction with Germany problematic but there are, after all, methods now already traditional for dealing with that situation. Germany's competitors in trade may complain. But German trade expansion alone could never create a serious political threat.

The position is, however, that in Latin America Germany limits herself to trade as little as elsewhere. She is carrying out a very thorough policy of political permeation which creates a serious threat both to the interior stability of many Latin American countries and to the stability of international relations in the western hemisphere. Moreover, it is not a question of German expansion alone. In Latin America the three main powers of the anti-Comintern pact meet. There are countries such as the Argentine and Peru where Italian influence predominates. Others such as El Salvador are Japanese strongholds. And some of these countries are mainly the object of German permeation.

It is difficult to distinguish clearly between the activities of these three powers. At present, at least, in South America much more than anywhere else, they act in close alliance. And there co-operation is much more untroubled than, for instance, that between Germany and Italy in the Mediterranean. The joint penetration of Latin America, though never very strongly emphasized, is not the least

among the objects of the anti-Comintern pact. Whether this totalitarian friendship will last in the long run is another question. Italian
influence in due course may become tributary to German influence.
But it is difficult to see how German and Japanese interests should
not clash eventually.

Both Germany and Japan are still too weak in the regions where
their interests conflict to compete seriously against each other in political influence. At present only German and Japanese tentacles
meet in India. And in South America, where the action of both
powers is already stronger, they must still combine in their attempts
to overcome the resistance of the United States. But in the western
as in the eastern hemisphere Germany meets Japan as the only
competitor she really regards as an equal. Accordingly, in the best-
informed German circles, interest for everything Japanese is very
strong.

But in the present study we must limit ourselves to German policy
in Latin America alone, somewhat artificial as is its separation from
Japanese and Italian policy in that area. The question arises: Why
does Germany really make such efforts in Latin America?

One reason undoubtedly is rooted in European affairs, in the
hostility of Germany towards Britain. Germany has not forgotten
the lessons of the last War. She rightly suspects that in a European
conflict the United States may prove in the end to be the decisive
factor. And she wants in this way to create trouble for the United
States nearer home so as to make it more difficult for her to interfere
in the Old World. This, like so many other lines of German policy,
is only a continuation of her policy during the War. Even in 1916
Germany attempted to draw Mexico into war with the United States
in order to prevent American intervention in France. What Germany is doing at present is partly a repetition of that policy on a
larger scale.

It is a dangerous game. By threatening the United States in her
own sphere of influence, Germany may bind the American forces
but is sure at the same time to rouse anger against herself which may

precipitate a more active policy on the part of the United States in Europe. Such has in fact already been the case. But Germany hopes to counterbalance that effect by stimulating the rise of Fascist and semi-Fascist movements in the United States which would follow a pro-German policy, and she places her hopes upon the next presidential elections and the possible victory of the isolationists.

But a tactical thrust against the United States is probably not the decisive motive behind German political expansion in Latin America. Something deeper and more general lies behind that. General Haushofer and the school of "geo-politicians" he leads, who wield such influence in German foreign politics, insist on the impossibility of Germany's remaining a purely continental power, meaning by "continental" not a power limited to the European continent but a power limited in the main to action on land. Germany is admittedly aiming at becoming a "world power," and she cannot become that without being at the same time a land and a sea power. Even at this early stage of German expansion, while Germany still accepts restrictions in naval construction, she aims at breaking through the "continental narrowness" which, according to Haushofer, would be her doom.

None of Germany's aims, as so far described, can truly be regarded as transoceanic. South Africa and India are transoceanic possessions for the British Empire, but in the German Empire they would be linked to the mother country by land-route. South America, from the German point of view, is truly transoceanic, and an extension of the German Empire to these parts would give Germany the standing of a real world power in her own eyes.

Besides, and this is probably the main reason for the German drive in Latin America, the countries concerned are an ideal field for German permeation. All the other tropical and sub-tropical countries, with one or two exceptions, are colonies or at least definitely dependent on one of the major powers. Only Latin America consists of independent republics, and belongs to none outside herself. At the same time most of the Latin American republics have not reached such a state of development where it would be very difficult for a strong modern power to permeate them. In every other part of the world, with the exception of the south-east of Europe, Germany must be prepared to fight some other power in order to gain possession. Latin America is the only area outside Europe where she can intrude entirely by indirect means. Thus Germany has thrown herself eagerly upon this relatively virgin field of colonial expansion.

Let us begin our analysis of German penetration into Latin America with a few general figures about the progress of German trade in those parts. Germany's share per hundred in the imports of some Latin American countries developed as follows:

	1913	1929	1933	1937
Argentine	16.9	11.5	10.0	10.3
Brazil	17.5	12.7	12.0	23.9
Chile	24.6	15.5	11.4	26.0
Colombia	14.1	14.4	17.8	13.4
Guatemala	20.3	14.2	12.3	32.4
Mexico	13.1	8.0	12.3	15.6
Peru	17.3	10.0	10.3	18.7
Uruguay	15.5	10.2	8.6	11.1
Venezuela	14.4	9.2	11.4	13.6

Germany's share in exports per hundred to these countries was as follows:

	1913	1929	1933	1937
Argentine	12.0	10.0	7.7	6.8
Brazil	14.0	8.8	8.2	17.1
Chile	21.5	11.0	6.9	9.5
Colombia	9.4	2.1	5.0	12.6
Guatemala	53.0	39.8	35.5	17.4
Mexico	5.5	7.6	9.6	9.4
Peru	6.7	6.1	7.7	13.7
Uruguay	19.5	14.9	14.8	13.2
Venezuela	18.9	4.7	1.4	2.4

These figures reveal certain interesting aspects. Most important among them, perhaps, is the fact that of the economically most important countries of Latin America the Argentine can hardly be regarded as a sphere of German economic influence. Incidentally, in this as in many other cases, the figures for 1938 will be rather more unfavourable to Germany, owing to the international trade recession and the decline in the purchasing power of the countries concerned. The Argentine in the political sense is as little a German zone of influence as a commercial one.

In addition to little Guatemala, the most important German position both in imports and exports is Brazil, where the figures still improved for Germany in the first half of 1938. For some years German imports headed the list for that country as also for Chile. But in Brazil this position was lost again to the United States in the second half of 1938. For reasons soon to be discussed, there is an assumption that Germany in 1939 may become the greatest importer from Mexico. In all other countries Germany's trade position is not yet paramount and bears no comparison to her position in the Balkans, where she usually takes between forty and sixty per cent of the products of the countries concerned.

Besides, the trend both of German exports and of imports as expressed in percentages is anything but uniform. It is true that the absolute figures until 1937 rose practically everywhere, but in a number of cases the German share has lagged behind that of other countries. This is due to many reasons. The Germans since 1933 have captured South American markets as it were by surprise, with the help of intensive propaganda, undercutting their competitors with the help of large State subventions, forcing their imports upon countries as a condition of taking their exports, etc. In this process Britain was far more severely hit than the United States, though it is true that certain German goods compete seriously with American products. Thus the sale of German motor cars from 1936 to 1937 rose from 764 to 1835 in the Argentine, from 1172 to 1906 in Brazil, from 73 to 774 in Uruguay, and accordingly in other Latin American countries. Office supplies are another item where Germany competes keenly with the United States. But on the whole German trade has done no harm to American business, while severely hitting British exporters.

But now these exporters are making serious efforts to retrieve their losses while the United States is taking measures against the German commercial threat. At the same time Germany is now up against the results of her own trade policy, the dissatisfaction of Latin American countries with the blocked accounts in so-called "Aski" marks (blocked marks solely for trade between Germany and South American countries), against the passive balance of trade with Germany enforced upon many South American countries, etc. Latin American Governments are now in some cases making efforts themselves to cut down trade with Germany. We shall see one dramatic instance of this in the case of Brazil. Undoubtedly the German market is essential for many South American products. Yet the position is not so hopeless as in the case of the Balkans, where Germany often can simply dictate her conditions. There are, in Latin America, very important competitors.

The net commercial advantage for Germany has nevertheless been considerable. In absolute figures, German exports to and imports from Latin America (in million Reichsmarks) developed as follows:

	Imports	Exports
1932	443.8	235.1
1933	284.6	286.1
1934	419.3	265.5
1935	546.5	290.8
1936	534.5	508.5
1937	850.1	652.1
1938	809.7	622.7

The figures for 1938 are in a way misleading because they refer to the old Reich only. They reveal the trend of a recession of German trade, but owing to the German conquests in Europe, the absolute figures were still rising. Generally speaking, the figures show how extremely advantageous South American trade has been for Germany.

But in South America, less than in many parts of the world, German trade is the decisive factor. There is one exception, the case of Mexico, because there trading with Germany released the Government from very serious political difficulties. Everywhere else, it is German political permeation which constitutes the dominant aspect of the German advance.

In the early stages, Germany concentrated her efforts upon Brazil. Brazil has always been one of the most conservative of South American countries. It is the largest and most important power in the Latin American world. Last, it contains a German minority of many more than one million, concentrated mostly in the south, in the states of Santa Catharina and Rio Grande do Sul, and intensely nationalist.

Getulio Vargas, the Brazilian president, holds extremely authoritarian views and was glad to accept German backing. Things came to a head in the usual South American manner on the occasion of the re-election of the president. In November 1937 Vargas, feeling himself insecure and his tenure of office threatened, abolished by *coup d'état* the constitution and proclaimed himself dictator. The Germans thought that they were very near winning out completely in Brazil.

It is very difficult to see through the intrigues which preceded and followed that *coup*. At any rate, the *coup* itself was supported to a degree by a totalitarian party, the Integralists. The leader of the Integralists was not Vargas but a certain Salgado. The movement differed from Nazism in certain ideological aspects. In Brazil, where practically every race in the world is represented, and where all freely intermingle, the idea of race purity must seem fantastic. The Integralist programme does not envisage any race purity but on the contrary an amalgamation of races in order to create a specifically Brazilian type. But as, at the same time, the Integralists are very anti-Semitic, the Nazis need not mind very much the dark spots of Integralist dogma.

The main impulse behind Brazilian Integralism is an extreme
form of that hostility against western influences, both economic and
cultural, which at present is sweeping all Latin America. As in other
Latin American countries, so in Brazil the young nationalists hate
the United States, Britain, and France which have invested capital
in this country and determined its cultural physiognomy. "Out with
foreigners" is the slogan. Yet the Integralists look to Germany, Italy,
and Spain for inspiration.

As a matter of fact, the Brazilian Integralists are the only movement in South America which can be regarded as properly Fascist
in any real sense of the word. Dictatorships are the most common
forms of government in South America, but not every dictatorship
is Fascist. In fact most of the so-called "revolutions" in South America are carried out without any participation by the masses. And
where, as in Mexico and Peru, there have been real mass movements,
they have been revolutions of the Left and not of the Right. In most
Latin American countries, feudal remnants and race cleavage create
much too large a gap between the classes (which at the same time
constitute different races) to allow of the formation of a unified
national movement. Latin American dictatorships, therefore, are
never in any real sense totalitarian. The dictator may be master of
the State machinery. But the State machinery is hardly ever the real,
complete master of the country. The influence of the Catholic Church
and, even more, the enormous distances and bad communications
make any ideological regimentation a thing beyond possibility. And
in the economic field, the countries concerned must be only too happy
if they find a sufficient amount of uncontrolled individual initia-
tive. The Fascist ideas borrowed by various Latin American dicta-
tors are only a thin veneer over entirely different systems of government.

The case of the Brazilian Integralists, however, is different. This
is probably due, in part at least, to the absence of any colour line in
Brazil. Here the struggle of the natives against foreign influence
does not coincide, as in Mexico, with the struggle of the coloured

people against the white inside their own country. Some measure of national unity can therefore be achieved in Brazil.

At any rate, the establishment of dictatorship, not only by way of fact but in principle, appeared to the Integralists as a prelude to the establishment of their own totalitarian ideal. There was a good deal of naïveté in that calculation. Vargas is a typical Latin American *caudillo,* caring for his personal rule and nothing else. After having achieved power, he had no intention of giving it up in favour of the Integralists. Disappointment led to a desperate determination on the part of the latter, and in May 1938 an Integralist rising against Vargas broke out in Rio de Janeiro. By surprise, it scored a considerable initial success, but was defeated after a few hours. It proved that in reality even the Integralists are something very different from a true Fascist party. There had been little undermining of the position of the Government from within, and the Integralists had thoroughly misunderstood the Fascist method of seizing power with no actual use of arms or very little. Theirs was an armed rising in the typical South American manner, prepared in secret and executed by a small group, with the general indifference of the masses.

The Germans themselves had been misled by the analogy between Integralism and Nazism and had backed the wrong horse. They had heavily supported Salgado, who had made the German colonies in Santa Catharina his stronghold. Thus the Integralist rising in one single day spoiled for Germany the results of many years of tenacious effort. From that moment onward, relations between Brazil and Germany have become clearly hostile.

Official Brazilian statements accused Germany of having helped in engineering the rising, and a number of representatives of German firms were arrested on a charge of high treason. German diplomatic intervention led to the release of the men in jail and to a recantation of the Brazilian Government in the matter of German complicity in the rising. But Vargas did not let himself be stopped in his measures against the German community in Brazil. That community, under very strong pressure, had been rigidly organized on Nazi lines and was now forcibly broken up. Not only were their political and cultural organizations dissolved, even their private schools were closed. Worst of all, the Government initiated a drive to break up the German settlements themselves and has attempted to scatter the German colonists all over the country. Under such pressure there began a significant movement of Germans of Brazilian nationality back to Germany.

Consequences in the commercial field were no less serious. Despite her brilliant position in Brazilian trade, or rather as a consequence of the methods by which she had acquired that position, Germany had aroused a great deal of ill-feeling among the economic leaders of the country. It was therefore easy for Vargas to strike back at Germany in the sphere of finance. In June 1938 Germany owed Brazil not less than forty to fifty million Aski marks. (As usual, it is impossible to convert this figure into dollars because Aski marks can be used only for the purchase of German goods and have no value on the open market.) At that moment the Brazilian National Bank stopped all financial transactions with Germany pending the recovery of the German debts. After a month of nervous negotiating, a new agreement was reached. Brazil, after all, could not in the long run dispense with the German market. It is not so much coffee, Brazil's staple product, which matters in German-Brazilian trade relations, but cotton and cocoa. Brazil has made serious efforts to get away from her one-crop agricultural policy, but could hardly have developed other crops, and especially cotton, without an outlet in Germany. Yet in the renewed trade agreement Brazil obtained exemption from the Aski-mark system for her cotton and cocoa. These two products have since been paid for in free exchange.

Thus Brazil is one of the few countries which so far have pushed back the German advance very successfully. While taking full advantage of the German market, Brazil has avoided becoming economically subservient to Germany and at the same time has got rid of German political intrigues in a very thorough manner. In the field of international affairs, the United States is the principal beneficiary of this development.

But if Brazil is an instance of successful resistance, Mexico is an instance of extremely successful German penetration. German efforts in Mexico have been continuous since the advent of the Nazis and have been little hampered by the revolutionary character of the Mexican Government. German propaganda simply disregarded the "Marxist" character of the Mexican revolution and maintained that both Germany and Mexico had achieved their national revolution and ought therefore to be allies. The very strong anti-foreign and anti-Yankee feeling prevailing in certain sections of Mexican public opinion gave this propaganda a chance. And in the context of enmity against the foreigners, even German anti-Semitic propaganda went off all right. In a conflict with the Anglo-Saxon powers, Mexico would obviously welcome any ally.

Yet in the purely political sphere the effect of this propaganda was limited. Germany was still too far off to be very valuable as an ally. More important, the Mexican Government is too emphatically "anti-Fascist" to be likely to collaborate closely with Germany, though the weight of these ideological antagonisms ought not to be overrated. Mexico is living under a dictatorship which might quite well evolve on totalitarian lines, and it would then make little difference whether or not the Government described itself as anti-Fascist. Yet, the slogan of anti-Fascism has its importance in German-Mexican relations under a different aspect.

While trying to convince certain elements in the Government camp, the Germans at the same time did not refrain from supporting adversaries of the Government who are generally though inaccurately described as "Fascists." Outstanding among them was General Cedillo, the governor of the state of San Luis Potosí in the north. President Cárdenas, with great energy, forestalled an imminent rising of this governor, which was intended to be a counterpart to the Franco rising in Spain. Public opinion was agreed that the Germans had had their fingers in this pie. And when Cedillo's rising collapsed right at the beginning, German prestige was involved.

Yet Nazi Germany has always contrived to collaborate with two hostile factions at once. In Mexico there were special reasons why they could strongly influence Cárdenas while conspiring with Cedillo. Germany had helped the Mexican Government in its difficulties over oil.

This is not the place to discuss the implications of the conflict of the Mexican Eagle and of other oil companies with the Mexican Government. One thing is certain: the development of the conflict has brought to light how extremely dangerous it is at present for big democratic countries to take strong action against their smaller neighbours. For the result of Anglo-American action in Mexico was to call the Germans in. The taxes imposed upon the oil companies may have been unbearably high, as those companies maintained, or acceptable, as was the view of observers friendly to the Mexican Government. But at any rate Sir Henri Deterding and his colleagues felt sure that in case of a rupture they would not be the losers, because the Mexican Government would be unable to sell and to ship the oil it had expropriated. And this would in fact have been true had there still existed that solidarity of the "capitalist" powers which fifteen years before had prevented the Russians from getting foreign loans at terms acceptable to them. But in the meantime Fascism had arisen.

Germany was not interested in English and American claims. She needed oil badly. She would be able to strike a favourable bargain with Mexico, and at the same time, by helping the Mexican Government out of its difficulties, would get a hold over it. This would secure further oil supplies and a fine stronghold in the western hemisphere.

The oil companies had calculated that even in case of Mexico's finding buyers the companies would have a sufficiently strong hold over the oil-shipping interests to make oil transport impossible. What actually happened was that an American firm, W. R. Davies, contracted with the Mexican Government for the delivery of a very considerable amount of oil of which by far the greater part went to Germany and most of the rest to Italy. Transport was largely carried out by Japanese tankers, and the German navy in 1938 was largely fuelled with Mexican oil. In the course of the negotiations, the agreement assumed ever wider proportions. The first amount mentioned was two million barrels, but soon increased to twelve million and finally to seventeen million barrels, of which fifteen million were actually delivered to Germany in 1938. Mexican oil production in 1937 had been twenty-five million barrels, so that only ten million remained for the Mexican Government to place, and of these a considerable amount went to Italy and other countries. It is true that the output of Mexican oil in 1937 was only a quarter of what it had been in 1921, but at any rate the plan of the oil companies had been defeated. As a result, it is expected that in 1939 Germany will hold first place in Mexico's imports. She is delivering to her in barter against oil, heavy machinery, equipment for irrigation, agriculture, and refineries, typewriters, office equipment, cameras, etc.

With that move, German influence in Mexico has become a serious matter and is probably bound to grow. Mexico is perhaps the only case where, owing to the special policy of the oil companies, German trade methods have worked entirely in favour of German political influence.

But German influence in Mexico is as nothing compared with German influence in the small republics of Central America. Guatemala must definitely be regarded as a German zone of influence, with the local dictator imitating Nazism to the best of his ability and Germany predominating in trade. The situation in Honduras is not very different, and El Salvador, under the ruthless rule of President Martínez, is a real stronghold of joint German and Japanese influence. The manager of the State-owned Farm Loan and Mortgage Bank is himself a German, while Italy provides aeroplanes and trains pilots. German purchases from El Salvador are infinitesimal as com-

pared with American purchases, yet the political trends are heavily
against the United States. German and Japanese penetration in Nica-
ragua has not yet gone quite so far but is growing. These almost un-
noticed little backward republics constitute a serious danger spot in
view of the proximity of the Panama Canal and of the possible effect
of events there upon Mexico. The law of the German advance in
these parts of the world is simply that it is strongest where resistance is weakest. That applies equally to the northern part of South
America. Thus Colombia is resisting German influence quite successfully, whereas in Ecuador it is growing because of the success
of German trade. Peru, farther south, is an Italian preserve, but in
Chile German influence is strong again owing largely to the strong
colonies of German settlers. It has, however, suffered a severe setback by the recent election of a Popular Front candidate to the presi-
dency.

Summing up this complex picture, a few conclusions emerge. In
trade, Germany, all over Latin America, is a serious competitor to
Britain but only a slight nuisance to the United States. In politics
it is the other way round. German, Italian, and Japanese intrusion
constitute a very serious threat to the Pan-American good-will policy
of the United States, and the effect of this intrusion in case of a large
international conflict would be quite incalculable. Certainly South
America would not again be a quiet backwater in the turmoil. Yet
the usual German methods of penetration are not fully applicable
in South America owing to Germany's incapacity to exert a physical
threat to any adversary in that area. That was very clearly brought
out in the German Brazilian conflict.

All Latin America, from the Rio Grande to Cape Horn, is swept
with German news, German radio, German whispering campaigns,
German goods, and German advice. Yet no Government in that
continent need give up its free hand to Germany. They all are under
the spell of the United States. Under these circumstances it is probably safe to say that German influence in Latin America both in
trade and in politics will decline wherever the large democracies take

serious counteraction. Given such action, Fascist penetration into Latin America will not constitute more than a second-rate influence. Without it, it might be very serious even at the present stage.

All this would be different once Germany had won domination over the European continent and broken up the British Empire. Then the threat to the United States by way of Latin America would become very strong and dangerous indeed. But at present this is only a dream.

CHAPTER XII

CONCLUSION

Even in this short survey certain general aspects of German expansion have come quite clearly to the surface, so that we have merely to repeat a few conclusions which are scattered through our text. Two facts are outstanding. German expansion is unlimited in its aims; it moves in the direction of the weakest resistance much more than in the direction of some definite object. But its final aim is world domination. This advance in the direction of weakest resistance links the first aspect of German expansion (its lack of limited aims) to the second: German expansion is primarily political, and economic in the second place. The military aspect, at least at present, does not generally operate directly but only as a potential threat.

This is tantamount to saying that Nazi expansion is primarily an attempt at a Fascist world revolution stimulated and backed by Germany. Here, and only here, lie Germany's chances. If all the countries threatened by her united against her, she would be crushed by overwhelming force. She sets her hope in a disintegration of her adversaries, in the supposed decline of democracy and in the revolt of the more mature colonial and semi-colonial nations against the old empires. However much she may lure her potential enemies into temporary alliances, a fight along ideological fronts is the mainstay of her policy. She could never, in the long run, put up with the existence of a democratic country. The breaking of the power of Britain, France, and the United States is therefore her main aim.

Taken in itself, such a scheme of world revolution may hold out splendid prospects. The disintegration of all existing political forms is in fact considerable. German use of main force seems to play merely the role of the midwife who sets the revolutionary forces free. And the result might conceivably be a commonwealth of Fascist na-

165

tions under German and Japanese guidance, built upon ideological unity and economic division of labour.

But this ideal picture does not hold good in practice. It is not only that the old powerful democracies cannot expect anything but disaster from such a scheme. The small nations which Germany wants to unite in a revolt against the old large countries are bound to suffer as much or more. For there are forces inherent in Fascism of both a psychological and an economic character which make it unfit as a balanced and durable form of government. Germany may cleverly use the interests and ambitions of others for the disintegration of her adversaries, but once she comes to the establishment of her own empire she quickly turns from a policy of co-operation between herself and her subject countries to a policy of ruthless oppression and exploitation. It is probably safe to say that for such a policy she cannot be strong enough in the long run. Putting the same idea in broader terms: no power could ever be strong enough for such a policy. Even the Romans and Persians ruled their vast empires with a large measure of local self-government and their rule took account of the legal, moral, and religious traditions of their subjects. An empire which rules entirely by force is the worst of horrors. But fortunately the worst of horrors can never last for long, even if it succeeds for a time.

There is no use denying that the German ideal of a Fascist world revolution is a challenge to our whole western civilization. If the challenge succeeds, it will not be due to overwhelming force of arms, but to the weakness of the moral, religious, and political impulses of the opposing side. That such weakness exists is the basic assumption of the German game, and, to a degree, it is an undeniable fact. But whether resistance to Fascism will in the end collapse, or whether values which have become somewhat time-worn acquire new vitality in the struggle against Fascism, only the future can show. But even if it collapses, the German sweep will probably have no more than a disruptive and disintegrating effect. Unreason in history is always followed by reason. Revolutions, after a period of violent reaction, end in some sort of stability. But it is never the revolutionaries themselves who establish the new stable regime. It is impossible to say how far the Fascist world revolution will go. But it is certain that its heirs will not again be Fascist. Even if Nazi Germany sweeps half the world or more, she will in the end collapse, owing to her inherent instability. She would then have been the pace-maker for some other regime not yet discernible.